Other Women

Other Women

The History of the Mistress

FIONA McDONALD

For Carl

First published 2013

The History Press
The Mill, Brimscombe Port
Stroud, Gloucestershire, GL5 2QG
www.thehistorypress.co.uk

© Fiona McDonald, 2013

British Library Cataloguing in Publication Data.
A catalogue record for this book is available from the British Library.

ISBN 978 0 7524 6538 8

Typesetting and origination by The History Press
Printed in Great Britain

Contents

Introduction

There once was a man from Lyme
Who kept three wives at a time
When asked, 'Why a third?'
He replied, 'One's absurd
And bigamy, sir, is a crime'.

Well, how does the lusty male avoid the sin of bigamy? He takes a mistress, or two, of course. The keeping of a mistress is a serious business and quite often one of considerable expense. Having a mistress is not like having a casual love affair, nor is it like visiting a prostitute who is paid only for her immediate sexual (and certainly not exclusive) services.

On the contrary, the woman who is taken to be a mistress must be housed, fed and clothed in a suitably comfortable, if not luxurious, manner. Offspring resulting from such a union must be acknowledged in some manner in order to compensate for their illegitimacy and they too must be provided for and educated. It is necessary for the man who wishes to keep a mistress to have the income to do so.

The relationship between a man and his mistress is an interesting one. It can simulate the married state almost exactly, lacking only the marriage vows and legitimacy for any offspring from the union. It can provide companionship with a partner of one's own choosing who may well share interests and intellect that are lacking in a spouse who was chosen for her wealth or social standing.

Becoming the mistress of a wealthy man could mean a safe and secure life for a woman and the children she has with him. For some women, sometimes already married with wealth and status, becoming the mistress of a king meant access to power and influence at court.

Women have been kept as mistresses by men for as long as there has been the institution of marriage. Sometimes the women are kept in a comfortable state for their lifetime, even after they no longer have a romantic or sexual relationship with the man who provides their living. On the other hand, mistresses can be cast aside when a new, younger or more beautiful woman takes a man's fancy – and then the rejected lover must either fend for herself as best she can, take up a profession (in some cases the man supplies the money for her to set herself up in business) or she is tossed away like a piece of refuse unless she finds another man to take her as his mistress.

This book does not attempt to delve into the morals of keeping women as mistresses nor does it judge whether it is a form of exploitation by either party. It will simply look at the stories of women who have been mistresses, and will occasionally sympathise with some of the sadder cases.

There are the tales of women who have been the lovers of kings, dukes and princes. There are women who supplied inspiration to artists and writers. And there are ordinary women who never expected more than a steady husband.

These are stories about individual women who chose or were chosen to follow a separate path from the socially respectable one of marriage, children and fidelity. Their lives were different from their married, faithful sisters and because of this they offer the reader a glimpse of another reality – with all its passion, intrigue and sadness.

Timeline

Providing a timeline will help to put these histories into perspective. Some stories will overlap and a timeline can help to give an overview at a glance.

1025 Possible birth date of Edith the Fair
1066 Battle of Hastings and death of Harold Godwin
1491 Birth of Henry VIII
1534 Henry declares himself supreme head of the Church of England
1547 Death of Henry VIII
1630 Birth of Charles II; birth of Lucy Walter
1640 Birth of Barbara Villiers
1648 Birth of Moll Davis
1649 Birth of Louise de Kérouaille
1650 Birth of Nell Gwyn
1658 Death of Lucy Walter
1661 Charles II crowned King of England
1685 Death of Charles II
1687 Death of Nell Gwyn
1708 Death of Moll Davis
1709 Death of Barbara Palmer (*née* Villiers)
1734 Death of Louise de Kérouaille
1756 Birth of Maria Smythe
1757 Birth of Georgiana Spencer, later Duchess of Devonshire
1758 Birth of Mary Darby
1759 Birth of Elizabeth Hervey Foster, later Duchess of Devonshire
1762 Birth of George IV

1778   Death of Charlotte Spencer, mistress of the Duke of Devonshire
1800   Death of Mary Robinson (*née* Darby)
1806   Death of Georgiana Spencer, later Duchess of Devonshire
1807   Birth of Harriet Taylor
1824   Death of Elizabeth Hervey Foster, later Duchess of Devonshire
1829   Birth of Elizabeth Siddal
1830   Death of George IV; birth of Caroline Graves
1837   Death of Maria Fitzherbert (*née* Smythe)
1839   Birth of Ellen 'Nelly' Lawless Ternan
1845   Birth of Martha Rudd
1858   Death of Harriet Taylor
1862   Death of Elizabeth Siddal
1879   Death of Claire Clairmont
1891   Birth of Freda Dudley Ward
1894   Birth of Edward VIII, later Duke of Windsor
1895   Death of Caroline Graves
1905   Birth of Thelma Morgan Furness
1914   Death of Ellen 'Nelly' Lawless Ternan
1919   Death of Martha Rudd
1970   Death of Thelma Morgan Furness
1972   Death of Edward VIII, later Duke of Windsor
1983   Death of Freda Dudley Ward

Part 1
The Place of a Mistress

DEFINING THE TERM MISTRESS

Prostitutes, concubines, whores, courtesans, lovers, mistresses are all terms that have been used interchangeably over the centuries to mean a woman who is having a sexual liaison with a man she is not married to, often with some kind of exchange of money or goods for services rendered. However, this does not mean that the terms used do not have very precise meanings.

Prostitute and whore: a person who has sexual intercourse for a fee. There is not necessarily any emotional bond between the couple although some prostitutes have regular clients. Some prostitutes work on the street, relying on casual passers-by for custom. Usually there is an unofficial specified area of a city or town where it is known that prostitutes ply their trade. A whore is another name for a prostitute but has a rather malicious connotation. To call someone a whore is usually an insult.

Courtesan: the word courtesan comes from courtier, a person who resides in the court of a monarch. Courtiers were not servants carrying out menial tasks but people of some social standing who would attend in various ways to the monarch. During the Italian Renaissance the word *cortigiana* meant the mistress of the king. A court mistress needed to have accomplishments to entertain her lover, usually a musical ability, dancing, intelligence and wit. In Italy there were two different classes of *cortigiana*. One had the word *onesta* applied to it (meaning honest), which referred to women of intellect, often from the aristocracy. The other had *di lume* (of light) after it and this was a lesser class of courtesan, although still considered higher than the street-walking prostitute.

The *cortigiane oneste* were not dissimilar to the ancient Greek *hetaerae*, who, although they did supply sex, were highly intelligent women who actively engaged in *symposia* (drinking parties) where philosophy and politics were discussed alongside art and poetry.

While many of their attributes seem similar to those of the mistress there seems to have been stricter guidelines for those working as courtesans. Traditionally, the less elevated courtesan was hired for company such as visiting dignitaries or special guests. She needed to be able to sing, dance and play the harp or harpsichord, or a similar instrument; she needed to be able to discuss a variety of subjects without being too opinionated. Courtesans could transfer or be transferred into the employ of another patron. Sometimes, when the woman's time of service was seen as coming to an end, possibly to do with age or perhaps because of a change in affection by her sponsor, she would have a husband found for her, suitable to her status: a bit like a retirement package. On the other hand, she could be flung out onto the streets to make her way as best she could, which was in many cases not very well.

In some cultures, courtesans were distinguished from other women (particularly at court) by the colours and cut of their dresses. And, as with royal mistresses, there was the opportunity for the courtesan to influence political decisions, or to spy on secrets. Also, there were rivalries and jealousies.

The male equivalent of the courtesan is known as a *cicisbeo* in Italian, *cortejo* or *estrecho* in Spanish, and *chevalier servant* in French. There is also the *gigolo*, a man who services women in the way that a high-class prostitute services a man.

Concubine: depending on the country in which these women lived their duties and status were quite different from one another. In China it was usual for an emperor or other high-ranking male to have a concubine, or several. Her position was lower than that of the wife but her children were all considered legitimate and could inherit their father's wealth and position (if male); the sons of the wife would, however, be considered socially superior. A concubine offered a good back-up plan for a man if his wife did not produce a male heir.

Just as with courtesans and mistresses, a concubine could rise up through the ranks until she became a formidable force and, if she was very clever, she could virtually rule the kingdom through her son.

Concubines, like their European counterparts, were often expected to be able to entertain guests as well as give their master sexual pleasure. Intellect was often highly valued, as was the usual dancing, singing and playing of music.

In ancient Rome the system was a bit different and was more in line with the idea of a mistress. A Roman male could take a woman to be his sexual partner (exclusively) if there was an impediment to the two marrying, such as the man was already married and/or the woman was of a lower social status.

A *concubinus* was slightly different. This was a way for a Roman male to have a male sexual partner without being considered homosexual. The *concubinus* was from the slave class. It was still considered necessary for the Roman to have a wife in order to beget offspring.

In America during the times of slavery, a system arose that was similar to that of ancient Rome. It was illegal for a white man or woman to marry a person of a different race (that is, from Africa or a Native American etc). To overcome this, men would sometimes take a slave to be their concubine. All children born to such unions were considered slaves by the law. This did not mean that there weren't happy relationships between masters and their slave concubines. It was up to the man to either provide comfort or love for his partner and their children or not. He was in a position to give his children an education, help them get on and later to free them.

In Louisiana yet another form of concubinage emerged that was called *placage*. Coloured women were given a dowry, property or something that would provide a certain status; their children with the man would get their freedom and the education that the children of a man of that standing would normally receive. It was far more a type of marriage than any of the other forms of concubinage or mistressdom.

Lover and mistress: a mistress is often thought to be a woman who is in a long-term relationship with a married man but who is faithful to him and often has children with him. She is sometimes called 'the other woman' or a 'kept woman'. The relationship is usually based on mutual attraction and is not always an agreement to have sex for money. A mistress can be a status symbol for a man; she may be highly desirable for her beauty or intelligence. Throughout history there are instances of women who are called mistresses who are not kept financially by the man they have this kind of relationship with. Sometimes the man, even though he might be a prince, for instance, is so short of money that it is the woman who keeps her own house and pays the bills. In such cases, there still can be an element in the relationship that requires the terminology of 'mistress', although 'love' can be interchangeable with this. For example, some of the stories in this book will defy the classification of the kept woman even though the women in question have been called mistresses in the history books.

MARRIAGE, DIVORCE AND SEPARATION

When Henry VIII wanted to rid himself of his first wife, Catherine of Aragon (to whom he had been married for almost twenty-four years) so that he could wed his mistress Anne Boleyn, the Pope in Rome forbade him. Thus Henry cited his incestuous relationship with Catherine – she had been his brother's wife and was a widow – and expected the Pope to use this as a mere formality to dissolve the union, as it was one of the two acceptable reasons for anulling a marriage. As it turned out, Henry had the Archbishop of Canterbury, Thomas Cranmer, annul his marriage to Catherine of Aragon on reasons of incest, just as he had asked the Pope to do. Henry also had his marriage to Anne Boleyn annulled on claims of incest and adultery, although she lost her head after being accused of treason.

The other acceptable reason for annullment was an inability to consummate the marriage and it is reported that Henry tried this excuse when he wanted to get rid of Anne of Cleves, claiming she was so ugly that he couldn't have sex with her. Yet why didn't Henry just divorce Anne? Because, although he had quarrelled and broken with the Roman Catholic Church and become head of the new Church of England, he had not implemented the institution of divorce. Many other Protestant countries in Europe had a divorce law in place by the mid-sixteenth century but Henry did not want his people following his lead and ditching their wives (or husbands) whenever they wished.

The fact remained that there were couples in England who no longer wanted to live together and who also wanted the freedom to remarry if the chance should come along. Other possibilities were to separate: to live in different dwellings and live independent lives. This could be an amicable arrangement but usually it involved lawyers drawing up documents of settlement on the wife by the husband, promising an allowance for her to live on. It also often meant that the father took the children with him. Custody was the right of the father, no matter how young the child. Married women at the time had no legal standing in the eyes of the law, so that when documents of separation were made it was between a husband and someone acting as trustee for his wife. This form of official declaration that a marriage was over, which throughout the eighteenth century became the most common form of marriage termination, still did not grant either party the right to remarry.

A party could just walk away from the marriage, disappear, flee back to the parental home or go into exile. A wife going to live elsewhere without her husband's consent could be ordered to return to him by the courts. Another popular way of ditching a wife was to sell her. This was not legal but that did not stop it happening. Sometimes the sale was by mutual consent, with the wife hoping to get a better deal.

Women had little say in any of the proceedings. One avenue open to her was the church courts. A woman could apply for separation from her husband if she could prove she was in danger from him physically or spiritually; she had to have two witnesses to every act she accused her husband of doing. The husband could also use these courts, although in contrast to women he did not have to prove anything. The church courts were, however, very expensive, the process was always drawn out and usually the outcome for a woman was not positive.

Things gradually improved for women. In 1839 the Infant Custody Act was brought in. This gave the courts the discretion of awarding custody of children under age 7 to their mother, unless the woman had been found guilty of adultery.

The Divorce Act was passed in 1857 and this meant that both men and women could apply for divorce, so that they could remarry. Men could ask for a divorce on the grounds of adultery but women had to prove that there had been cruelty, desertion, sodomy, bigamy or bestiality in the marriage. It was still an unfair system: men were more easily to succeed in their claims whereas women would inevitably be humiliated and blamed for the marriage breakdown – and the poor still did not have real access to divorce because it was too expensive, averaging £100 (about £4,300 in today's money).

The Matrimonial Causes Act was introduced in 1878. Yet it was nothing more than a theoretical attempt to make things more equal for women, which in practice generally did not happen. This act allowed a woman to ask for a legal separation from her husband on grounds of cruelty, such as being beaten. In practice, however, the plea was usually not granted. Several years later, in 1884, the punishment of imprisonment for a wife who refused to return to her marital home and resume 'conjugal rights' with her husband was abolished.

It was not until 1923 that men and women in England had equal rights in divorce cases, but it was more than another forty years before divorce could be granted for reasons of incompatibility.

Marriage was, until towards the last quarter of the twentieth century, a binding contract that was extremely difficult to break, particularly for women.

INHERITANCE AND PROPERTY RIGHTS

It wasn't until 1870, with the Married Women's Property Act, that women in England had a right to keep for themselves money they had earned during their marriage. Twelve years later, the act was amended to include all property. This meant that finally women had some means to look after themselves if a marriage failed.

Until the late nineteenth century any land or money that a woman brought with her into marriage automatically became the husband's property; married women, through the act of marriage, lost all legal status. It was stated that when a man and woman married they became a single unit. If this were truly thought to be the case then one could ask why the man was put solely in charge of income and property, as surely it should be handled jointly. One way around this was for the parents of the daughter to have legal documents drawn up explicitly stating that any money and inheritance that went with the daughter into marriage was to remain hers alone. This was an attempt to protect large estates from being squandered by a husband, and to give the woman an income if things didn't turn out.

When a man died his widow was granted independence. She could inherit her husband's estate and fortune, or his business or farm. Usually the estate went to the eldest legitimate son, but a substantial portion of his inheritance was settled on the widow as a pension.

Men, on the other hand, didn't have to wait for their wives to die in order to get their hands on any land or money that she brought with her into the marriage, they could have their wives put into asylums, claiming that they were mad – though in reality all it took was brute force. Women locked up in this way had little chance to defend themselves. It was extremely difficult to prove that the husband was in the wrong and it took a lot of effort by friends and family of the woman to get the King's Bench to issue a writ of *habeas corpus* so that the incarcerated wife could be granted her freedom.

However, as we know through the trials of Mr Rochester in Charlotte Brontë's *Jane Eyre*, a man of integrity was not at liberty to divorce his wife because she was truly insane. Marriage, unless under exceptional circumstances, was till death do they part, for better or worse, in sickness and in health.

Part 2
Mistresses of Royalty

For the kings of Europe from the Middle Ages right up until the late nineteenth century, it was a common custom to take at least one mistress, if not more, as a social, intellectual, romantic and sexual alternative to the legally wedded wife. Sometimes the arrangement suited both the king and his spouse: if the marriage had been made for political, economic or social reasons then the less sex she needed to have with him the better. Mostly the situation arose without any concern for the feelings of the wife, who was used as a breeding machine to bring forth the essential royal heir. This is not to say that there were no royal marriages in which the spouses didn't come to love each other. Charles I and his wife were such a pair; lovers as well as a diplomatic union.

For a woman chosen to be the mistress of a monarch or man in a high position it was an opportunity to influence decisions of state, to have a say in a normally male-dominated world. She could enjoy certain social freedoms, have stimulating intellectual conversations with men of letters and the arts, and could access all sorts of secrets of state.

Who were these women and what backgrounds did they come from?

There were those who were born with the right credentials, for instance the Boleyn sisters whose father was Thomas Boleyn, Earl of Wiltshire, Earl of Ormond and Viscount Rochford. Their mother was the daughter of the 2nd Duke of Norfolk. Mary was one of Henry's mistresses, a position later filled by her sister Anne. Anne's parentage was of sufficiently high social standing as to not be an impediment to the king eventually marrying her (there were, however, plenty of other reasons that were put forth).

One of Charles II's long-term mistresses was the actress Nell Gwyn. Her origins were not only obscure but were very low down the social scale and not of any social consequence. Therefore, even without the problem of there already being a queen at Charles's side, she would never have been considered marriageable, no matter how deeply the king loved her.

Nell's status was so unimportant that when the king tired of her he had her installed at a house belonging to the Crown but to which she was only a lessee. Nell indignantly asserted herself and demanded the title of the property be made over to her. The sole survivor of Nell's two sons by the king, and named Charles in his honour, was given the title Earl of Burford, later to become the Duke of St Albans.

There are too many stories to tell in this book about all the mistresses to all the kings of England. Added to this, there are even more intriguing stories about mistresses to monarchs across the sea. This short list identifies some that might offer enticing stories for further study:

ENGLAND AND SCOTLAND:

Rosamund Clifford (before 1150–c.1176), also known as 'Fair Rosamund' or 'the Rose of the World', was mistress to Henry II.
Agnes Dunbar was mistress to David of Scotland from 1369–71.
Alice Perrers (c.1340–1400), mistress to King Edward III.
Elizabeth 'Jane' Shore (c.1445–c.1527), one of many mistresses to Edward IV and later to several other men.
Elizabeth Blount (c.1502–39/40), one of Henry VIII's long-term lovers and one he did not attempt to marry.
Mary Boleyn (c.1500–43), the first of the Boleyn sisters to become mistress to Henry VIII.
Anne Boleyn (c.1501/07–36), the second sister to become Henry VIII's mistress and later his wife.
Elizabeth Hamilton, Countess of Orkney (1657–1733), mistress to William III and II of England and Scotland from 1680–95.

Elizabeth Villiers, mistress to William III.
Arabella Churchill, mistress to James II.
Catherine Sedley, mistress to James II.
Ehrengard Melusine von der Schulenburg (1667–1743), mistress
  to George I.
Henrietta Howard, Countess of Suffolk, mistress to George II.
Mary Scott, Countess of Deloraine (1703–44), mistress to George II.
Amalie von Wallmoden, Countess of Yarmouth, mistress to George
  II from the mid-1730s to 1760.
Elizabeth Conyngham, Marchioness Conyngham, mistress to
  George IV.
Dorothy Jordan, mistress to William IV while he was the Duke of
  Clarence. They were together for twenty years and had ten children.
Lillie Langtry, mistress to Edward VII.
Daisy Greville, Countess of Warwick, mistress to Edward VII.
Lady Jennie Churchill (1854–1921), mistress to Albert Edward,
  Prince of Wales, later Edward VII.
Lady Frances 'Daisy' Brooke, later Countess of Warwick (1861–
  1938), mistress to Albert Edward, Prince of Wales, later Edward VII.
Alice Keppel (1869–1947), mistress to Edward VII.
Wallis Warfield Simpson, later Duchess of Windsor (1895–1986),
  mistress then wife to Edward David, Prince of Wales, King
  Edward VIII, later Duke of Windsor.

EUROPE:

Agnes Sorel (1421–50), mistress to King Charles VII of France.
Louise de la Valiere, mistress to King Louis XIV of France from
  1661–67.
Anna Mons, mistress of Tsar Peter the Great from 1691–1703.
Madame Du Barry, mistress of Louis XV of France.
Jeanne-Antoinette Poisson, Marquise de Pompadour, mistress of
  Louis XV of France.
Eliza Rosanna Gilbert, later Countess of Landsfeld, Irish dancer
  with the stage name 'Lola Montez', mistress of King Ludwig I
  of Bavaria.

Maria Antonovna Naryshkina (1779–1854), a Polish noble who was mistress to Tsar Alexander I of Russia for thirteen years.

Magda Lupescu, mistress to King Carol II of the Romanians.

Marie, Countess Walewski, a Polish noble who was mistress to Emperor Napoleon Bonaparte.

Caroline Lacroix, mistress to Leopold II of Belgium.

Baroness Mary Vetsera, mistress to the Crown Prince Rudolf of Austria (1871–89). Vetsera never had the opportunity to become the wife of Rudolf because they were found dead together in his hunting lodge. It was thought that it was a suicide pact. However, there are other theories …

EDITH THE FAIR

One of the earliest mistresses to be noted in English history may not really qualify for that title. Her name is Edith the Fair (*c.*1025–*c.*1086) and there are various versions of the spelling of this ancient name. She has also been called Edith Swan Neck and Edith the Gentle Swan. To say she was Harold Godwinson's mistress is probably to misunderstand the law and customs of the time in which they lived. As descendants of Danes they tended to hold on to traditions that had been brought from that country. One of these was hand-fasting, a commonly practised form of marriage. It was considered a legal form of marriage and the children from such a union were not seen as illegitimate. However, it was not seen as a proper marriage in the eyes of the Church.

Edith was born around AD 1025 and had been married to Harold II for a good twenty years before he died. They had five children that are known of: three boys – Godwin, Edmund and Magnus, and two girls – Gunhild and Gytha. Gunhild went into the convent at Wilton; Gytha married Vladimir Monomakh, Grand Duke of Kiev. She was always considered to be of royal stock.

Edith possessed land in her own right and is thought to be one of the earliest owners of Sheredes and Hodders Danbury Manor. It was here that Harold was supposed to have spent a last night with his wife before he went to battle with William the Conqueror.

Some time before Harold's last stand, he was fighting the Welsh under their leader Gruffydd ap Llewelyn. Harold was victorious and as part of a plan to unite Wales and Mercia, tying them to England, he took Llewelyn's widow, Ealdgyth, to be his queen consort by marrying her in church and in the sight of God. Why he had never married Edith in a church ceremony is not known; perhaps the two felt it was not necessary as they were bound together by their handfasting ceremony. Certainly Harold's second marriage was not made through love, although several accounts tell of Ealdgyth's incredible beauty. Rather, the marriage was a political device that meant it would be easier for Harold to control his former enemies. Ealdgyth was nothing more than a token to seal a bargain – and her thoughts and wishes did not come into it.

When Harold was killed at the Battle of Hastings his body was badly mutilated. The clerics sent to recover it could not identify it so, as the legend goes, Edith the Fair, Harold's long-time partner and the mother of his children, strode through the blood and gore and identified him by marks on his chest that were known only to her (romantic speculation claims they were the scars of love bites). Harold's queen, Ealdgyth, was collected by two of her brothers, who presumably took her back to the heart of her home and people.

THE MISTRESSES OF KING CHARLES II

The seventeenth century was notable for the commonality of keeping a mistress, whether it was due to a craze or because Charles II made it fashionable. In fact, it was almost a social requirement that

Charles II

a gentleman have a long-standing liaison with a woman who was not his wife. Apparently Francis North, Lord Guilford was a gentleman who was considered to have neglected his duty by not keeping a mistress.

CHARLES, THE MAN

If a monarch is born under the star of Venus is it any wonder that he often falls in love with beautiful women? King Charles II was born on 29 May 1630 under such a constellation and he certainly made it his business to love women.

Charles II had no children with his wife, Catherine of Braganza. She suffered several miscarriages and stillbirths. In spite of the fact that Charles had sired a number of illegitimate children with various mistresses, England's throne was to be handed to Charles's brother James upon the king's death.

THE MISTRESSES

Lucy Walter

Lucy Walter (*c*.1630–1658) is considered to be the first in a long line of Charles II's mistresses. She is the first to have had a child that Charles admitted as his own. Unfortunately, Lucy came into Charles's life when it was in turmoil. His royal father had been beheaded and he was in exile himself, and lacking regular funds. His attempt to win back the kingdom cost all of the money that his loyal supporters could scrape together; there was nothing left over with which to indulge a young woman with no dowry. Consequently Lucy's life as the would-be king's mistress was not a secure one and, when Charles went away on campaigns, Lucy was left without a provider. This meant that she was tempted to take other lovers, which did nothing to ensure trust and loyalty from Charles (he was not crowned king until 1661, long after his relationship with Lucy had fallen by the wayside).

Lucy Walter was born in the same year as Charles II. Her parents were Richard (or William) Walter of Roch Castle in Wales and

Lucy Walter

his wife, Elizabeth Protheroe. They were a noble family who were staunch Royalists during the Civil War, for which their property was seized and razed to the ground by the Parliamentarians. It is thought that Lucy was born in Wales, but moved to London in her childhood after the destruction of her family home. It is also a possibility that her parents had separated and that Lucy and her mother were living as best they could amongst other Royalists, in a state of upheaval.

Exactly what she did in her teenage years and with whom is largely conjecture. Samuel Pepys and Lord Clarendon have written that she had already indulged in a number of sexual affairs before she left England for Holland, by way of Paris, at age 18. One of her lovers was supposedly Algernon Sidney, second son of the Earl of Leicester and a Parliamentary supporter. After a fling with Algernon, Lucy is said to have moved on to the younger brother, Robert. Other sources say that Lucy went with Robert to The Hague, travelling under the adopted name Barlow. Yet another version is that Lucy was taken to Paris by an uncle and from there she found her way into Holland, where she had her initial encounter with Charles in exile.

Whichever story is true, the fact is that Lucy met Charles in The Hague in the year 1648 and had an affair with him. Charles left Holland not long after he and Lucy conceived a child. It was during this time that rumours arose about the possibility of the child's father being Robert Sidney, as it is believed that Lucy had a liaison with Robert during Charles's absence.

When Charles returned to The Hague he settled back into his relationship with Lucy, who bore their son James in 1649. Charles seemingly had no doubt that the child was his and later bestowed upon him the title of 1st Duke of Monmouth. Lucy and Charles remained a couple until he left for Jersey (Lucy may have accompanied him for part of that time) and then to Scotland in 1650. Alone in Holland, Lucy turned to other men to provide for her. To one of them she bore a daughter, Mary. When Charles finally returned he did not acknowledge the child as his and made it clear to Lucy that their relationship was truly at an end. There are sources that claim there were several intimate meetings between them after this, one even as late as 1656.

Lucy's life gradually deteriorated from then on. Charles did not give in to her constant demands for money and he tried hard to get custody of his son, by means fair or foul. At one point Charles tried to take the boy by force. A kidnapping was successful in 1658 and James was taken from his mother to Paris. Lucy, desperate to get her son back, followed him to France, but before she could find him she was taken ill and died. As she lay dying she told John Cosin, who would later become Bishop of Durham, that she was the legal wife of Charles II. This is a claim that Lucy had made several times throughout her life but there had never been any evidence to support it. Indeed, if there had been any truth in it then Lucy would have been in danger of committing bigamy – as it is known that she seriously contemplated marriage with Sir Henry de Vic. Given that Charles was ready to approve the match, it is unlikely that he and Lucy had ever been officially married.

The supporters of Charles's brother James, in their bid to see him succeed to the English throne, did everything they could to discredit James of Monmouth in order to lessen his claim to it. They even blackened his mother's name, claiming she was of low parentage and of no consequence. A memoir written by a member of the court of James II records that Lucy Walter died of syphilis, which may well have been a deliberate slur contrived to discredit her.

After Charles ended his affair with Lucy she did take on more lovers and it is possible that with such a promiscuous lifestyle she may have contracted venereal disease. One of her lovers was Lord Theobald Taffe, an Anglo-Irishman who was one of the exiled prince's main confidantes. Taffe was in all probability the father of Mary Walter, Lucy's daughter. It was Taffe to whom Charles appealed to ask that he urge discretion on Lucy in the aftermath of the couple's failed relationship. Taffe was to tell Lucy to leave The Hague, as it was too public and was in neither her interest nor Charles's that she was in such close proximity to him. Taffe was also entrusted with the duty to arrange a monetary allowance to keep Lucy and the children. Unfortunately Lucy had been the mistress of an exiled prince, not an established king, and money was never in great abundance or handed out regularly enough to keep her from accepting protection from other lovers.

A couple of years before her death Lucy took her two children back home to England. Whatever thought was behind the action, the result was that she was arrested by Cromwell. While imprisoned she was referred to both as Charles's wife and his mistress. The former title held no weight: it was not believed and she was released and allowed to return to Holland.

The diarist John Evelyn refers to Lucy Walters as a Mrs Barlow. He describes her as being brown and beautiful but insipid in nature. Later, after Charles II's death, Evelyn called her a strumpet, although he still remembered she had been beautiful. He claims Lucy was of low birth and that in his opinion there was certainly doubt as to the true paternity of her son James Monmouth. Pepys claims that he could see a strong resemblance to the younger Sidney brother. This may have been in response to the fact that Monmouth had been arrested and tried for treason against the king, for which he was executed.

Lucy Walter was unlucky to have lived in a time of turmoil, when Royalists were stripped of land and money – and becoming a mistress to one meant leaving oneself open to penury. If Lucy had managed to stay close to Charles until 1651 then she could have been the mistress to a king, and may well have managed to secure herself a lifetime's pension and comfort. Instead she was seen as nothing more than a nuisance to Charles, and his prospects, and he treated her with little regard even though she was the mother of his eldest son.

In 2012 DNA tests were made concerning James Monmouth. The results strongly suggest that Charles II was indeed his father.

Barbara Palmer (née Villiers), Countess of Castlemaine, Duchess of Cleveland

Barbara Villiers (1640–1709) was born into the gentry. Her father was William Villiers, the 2nd Viscount Grandison, who also happened to be a nephew to the Duke of Buckingham. Barbara's mother, Mary Bayning, was the daughter of the 1st Viscount Bayning and an heiress to her father's estate. As a staunch Royalist family there was no denying that Barbara had the right credentials to become the King of England's mistress.

As with many of the royal supporters during the time of England's Civil War, Barbara's family suffered many losses. First, her father used much of the estate's money to fund his part in the war, which left the family in reduced circumstances. Then he was killed at the

Barbara Palmer

Battle of Newbury in 1643; Barbara was only 4 years old. Not long after his death Mary Villiers married a cousin of her late husband's, Charles Villiers, 2nd Earl of Anglesey. The marriage may have provided some stability to the mother and daughter but money was still in very short supply. Charles Villiers, like his late cousin, was a Royalist and, after Charles I was executed in 1649, the family became supporters of the dead king's son.

Barbara Villiers was beautiful, clever and witty enough to attract many would-be suitors, until they discovered that she was almost penniless. At that time, not many men could afford to marry for love alone. Barbara's first paramour was Philip Stanhope, 2nd Earl of Chesterfield. Yet the match was not going to be anything more than a romance as Stanhope was in need of a wife with a good dowry.

At age 19 Barbara married Roger Palmer, 1st Earl of Castlemaine (this is the name that Barbara was often referred to by contemporary diarists of the time), who was a devout Catholic. The marriage was not to the liking of the groom's family; Roger's father told him that Barbara would make him a very unhappy man. He was not wrong. Barbara ended up having six children of whom it is thought that not one of them was Roger's.

As supporters of the exiled Prince Charles, Roger and his wife travelled to The Hague shortly after their marriage. It was here that Barbara met Charles and quickly became his foremost mistress. It was for services rendered (probably Barbara's not Roger's) that the title of Castlemaine was bestowed upon the couple in 1661 after Charles was restored to the throne.

When Charles II ascended the throne he was in want of a suitable wife. Kings, queens, princes and princesses rarely had a say in the lifelong partners chosen for them. Marriage was usually a political and economic business deal. Charles II married the Portuguese princess Catherine of Braganza. Barbara made sure that her second child with Charles was born at Hampton Court while the royal couple were on honeymoon.

Unlike poor Lucy Walter, Barbara Palmer was openly acknowledged as the king's mistress and was given the position of the Lady of the Bedchamber. The queen, knowing who and what Barbara was, argued strongly against the appointment. Yet her pleas were unheeded and Barbara was installed at the heart of the royal household. For the queen's defence there was at least one strong advocate, Edward Hyde, Earl of Clarendon who, as the king's adviser, spoke against Barbara's employment. The queen and her Lady of the Bedchamber did not become friends. Barbara made sure that the queen knew how things stood between herself and the king.

As Charles II took other mistresses his passion for Barbara declined. While she was still relatively young though, the flame would rekindle and, as a result, at least five children were born to Barbara and Charles.

In 1663 Barbara publicly announced her conversion to Catholicism. What her motives were are unclear. It is thought that she could have been trying to increase her influence with the Protestant king, who felt pulled towards Catholicism himself, or it may have been because of something to do with Roger Palmer, Barbara's estranged husband; whatever the reason it was certainly for personal gain.

Barbara Palmer enjoyed the status of being the king's mistress, she enjoyed the financial position it put her in and the titles she was able to claim through it. She was not averse to dabbling in politics either, though not that she had a large degree of sway in that area.

In 1670, at the age of 30, Charles II made Barbara a very handsome gift of Phoenix Park in Dublin and named her Baroness Nonsuch (a title to go with Nonsuch Palace, which she owned). It was well in the way of being a payoff for her long and faithful service. At 30, Barbara would have been considered old and the king had replaced her several times over. The young actress Nell Gwyn had replaced Barbara as Charles's favourite long-term mistress. In fact Barbara was asked to vacate her premises in the Whitehall Apartments so that the young Nell could be installed there. In 1672 Barbara produced a sixth child, another girl, but the king refused to name it as his own. This was a definite sign that sexual relations were over between them.

Barbara's position as royal mistress and insider came to an end in 1676. An Act of Parliament was passed making it illegal for a Catholic to hold office. The queen's hated Lady of the Bedchamber was sacked.

Barbara took her four youngest children and spent the next three to four years in Paris, where she took a number of lovers. In the last days of Charles's life it is recorded that he spent them in the company of three of his favourite women: Barbara, Nell and Louise de Kérouaille.

After Charles's death Barbara took up with some undesirable men, one of whom, Cardonell Goodman, an actor, she is supposed to have had a child with in 1686. In 1705 her husband Roger Palmer died and Barbara was free to marry again, which she did so with Major General Robert 'Beau' Fielding. The major was only after her fortune and, as he was already married, Barbara was able to prosecute him for bigamy. She died four years later in 1709 of dropsy.

Moll Davis

Moll (c.1648–1708) was an actress and singer born in Westminster, apparently illegitimately to Colonel Howard, 3rd Earl of Berkshire. Obviously her father did not think his connection with her was sufficient to have any kind of upbringing that would prepare her to be a lady. In the 1660s Moll joined the 'Duke's Theatre Company' and lived with the family of the manager, Sir William Davenant.

Charles II was a frequent theatregoer and it is likely that it was there that he first became acquainted with Moll. They began their affair in 1667 and Moll retired from the stage a year later. In 1669 Moll gave birth to a girl, Mary Tudor. The relationship between the king and Moll was not a long one. While she was one of his favourites she was showered with money and jewels, housed sumptuously, even sporting her own coach. A comfortable house full of furniture was provided for her in a street belonging to a nephew of Moll's father.

Why she fell out of favour is not really known, but it is popularly attributed to a rather nasty trick supposedly played on her by her rival, the actress Nell Gwyn. The story goes that Nell understood Moll was going to spend the night with the king so, in a fit of jealousy, laced Moll's food with jalap, well known for its laxative effects. Moll was not well that night and the symptoms put a halt to any thoughts of lovemaking.

Moll was well provided for even though she was no longer part of the king's retinue. She was given a lifelong annuity of £1,000 (around £83,000 today) and was able to retain her house. In 1673 Moll sold

Moll Davis

up and bought a large house in St James's Square for £1,800. Over ten years later she took her new husband, the composer James Paisible, to live in this house. Moll died in 1708.

Nell Gwyn

'Pretty, witty Nell' (1650–1687), as Samuel Pepys called her, was born in very low social circumstances, perhaps in Hereford, perhaps in Oxford, but more probably in Covent Garden, London. Her father may have been Captain Thomas Gwyn, a Royalist soldier, although this story was not popularly believed at the time. Nell's mother, on the other hand, was notorious as a vulgar, drunk madam of a brothel. Nell also had a sister, Rose. In 1663, Rose Gwyn was locked up in Newgate Prison on a charge of theft. She petitioned Harry Killigrew, son of the owner of the King's Theatre, to get her a pardon.

Nell and her sister worked first for their mother. It is rumoured that the girls both worked as prostitutes in their mother's brothel, although Nell later strenuously denied this. A new theatre was opened close to where the girls lived – The Theatre in Bridges Street – and Nell and Rose went to work for a former prostitute, Mary Meggs (known as Orange Moll) selling oranges, sweetmeats and other treats to theatregoers. It was in this capacity that Nell and her sister became acquainted with the theatre and acting.

At age 14 Nell, almost completely illiterate, began to take on small roles on stage. To see if she could live up to her promise, she attended acting classes conducted by Thomas Killigrew, who led the King's Company of players, and one of his leading actors, Charles Hart. Dancing was taught by John Lacy.

The parts Nell played grew more important and complex. The first documented evidence of Nell performing in a major role is in 1665. It was a play by Dryden, and Nell was given a serious part to play, though Pepys noted in his diary that she played it poorly. Nell admitted that she was much better at playing comic characters and it was in another play later in the same year that she starred in a comedy by James Howard, *All Mistaken, or the Mad Couple*. The actor Charles Hart played her onstage lover, a role that he was only too happy to continue in their private lives. The play was a success and the making of Nell as an actress.

Nell Gwyn

Nell's brilliant debut was cut short by the Great Plague, which saw all public places such as theatres being closed down to help stop the spread of the disease. Nell, her mother and a number of other actors and actresses left London for Oxford, along with the king's court. Charles II could not live without his entertainment and he had the players put on pieces for the court. The performers were granted the right to wear the king's livery and therefore be counted as his servants.

When the threat of the Plague was over, the theatre reopened and Nell continued her new and popular comic role as one half of a 'gay couple' (taking that word in its original sense). At this time Nell was having an amorous affair with Charles Sackville, Lord Buckhurst. The pair went on holiday to Epsom and Nell was supposed to have been paid an allowance by her lover of £100 (around £8,300) a year.

It wasn't until 1668 that Nell became a close part of Charles II's life. Charles was well acquainted with Nell as a performer but he got to know her more intimately when she sat in a theatre box beside his. They flirted throughout the performance and afterwards dined with Mr Villiers at a local coffee house. The story goes that when the bill had to be paid neither the king nor Mr Villiers had the cash to do so and Nell had to cover the cost for them all. Needless to say, she was a trifle underwhelmed but came up with a suitable sharp quip for the occasion.

It was not long after this episode that Nell was acknowledged at court as the king's mistress. She referred to her latest lover as Charles III because she had already had a fling with Charles Hart and then Charles Sackville, therefore the king had to be Charles III. Nell was determined to be faithful to her lover; she knew (although she didn't like it) that he would have more than one mistress at a time but she swore fidelity to him. It rankled that she had a rival in Moll Davis, and Nell supposedly helped Moll to fall out of favour (via her little trick with the purgative and the sweetmeats, as previously described).

Being the lover of a monarch did not prevent Nell from staying on the stage. She did take a break in 1670 for the birth of her first child, Charles Beauclerk, fathered by the king.

Nell might have been taken care of but the king soon brought in a new lady, Louise de Kérouaille. This French lass had a slight cast to one eye and Nell unkindly called her Squintabella. Perhaps it was to show the king her independence that Nell returned to the stage in 1671 for one more season, at the grand old age of 21. And maybe it was to appease her that he had her lodged in a townhouse close to the court. There must have been a reconciliation that year because Nell gave birth to a second boy, James.

One of the most appealing things about Nell Gwyn was her working-class background. She was the darling of the people because she represented them in her Englishness and her lack of aristocratic breeding. Nell had no airs whatsoever. She also had a ready repartee to protect herself from slights and insults, and was always happy to make fun of those whom she thought deserved it, drawing on her comic acting genius in which to do so.

Nell was not greedy for wealth and she did not want titles for herself, but she certainly felt that her two children deserved to have the same as the king's other bastards had: acknowledgement of their royal birth by means of titles and land. It was also not fair, she said, that because she was a commoner her house was only leased for her; she should be entitled to own it as other mistresses had before her. In 1676 the freehold on her house was granted to her and her sons were given titles: Charles was given the Earl of Burford and James, Lord Beauclerc. Little James didn't live to understand the full impact that his title would have given him. In 1671, while at school in Paris, he suddenly died. Nothing is known of the incident, although it was noted at the time that he had died of 'a sore leg'. Charles, on the other hand, was made Duke of St Albans in 1684 and made Chief Ranger of Enfield Chase and Master of Hawks, to be taken up when the positions next became vacant. The youth was also given a yearly allowance of £1,000.

The following year Charles II lay dying. He called his brother James to hear his last wishes. These included ongoing welfare for Barbara Palmer, Louise Kérouaille and Nell Gwyn. The king's words were recorded as being 'Let not poor Nelly starve'.

James probably wanted to put his brother's former lovers into a sack and throw them into the River Thames, but he did eventually put the requests into action. Nell was given £1,500 a year and her debts and mortgages were all paid off.

Nell Gwyn did not survive her Charles III by more than two years. She had a stroke in March 1687 followed by another in May. She died in November of that same year. The supposition is that she had a form of syphilis. Nell was not able to live within the means of her pension and when she died she had as many debts as ever. However, she managed to leave a bequest to the inmates of Newgate Prison to help ease their lives there.

Louise de Kérouaille, Duchess of Portsmouth

Louise de Kérouaille (1649–1734) was born to an aristocratic couple from Brittany. It is said that the family name, Kérouaille, was taken from a female ancestor who had married François de Penhoët in 1330.

As a girl Louise was sent to live with the family of Charles II's youngest sister, Henrietta Anne Stuart, the Duchess d'Orléans, married to the brother of Louis XIV. Louise accompanied Henrietta Anne on her trip back to England to visit Charles in 1670. Apparently Charles asked his sister if he could keep Louise for himself, but she told him the girl had been entrusted to her care and that the family would be expecting her to be looked after. There are rumours that Louise's family in fact sent her into the duchess's household in order that she be thrown in the way of a king, French or English, with a view to becoming the mistress of one of them.

The Duchess d'Orléans died of a sudden and violent illness a few days after her return to France. It was thought at first to have been caused by poison but has since been determined that a duodenal ulcer resulted in acute peritonitis and it was this that caused the intense pain that accompanied her death. Louise was in need of a home and employment and it was thought an excellent idea that she be offered to Charles II's wife, Catherine of Braganza, as a lady-in-waiting. Everyone knew what this really meant; a delicate morsel for the king himself. If there was any hint of Louise being a sacrificial lamb sent to the King of England as a means of keeping track of events, then she went with a willing spirit.

It did not take long for Louise to become a great favourite of Charles II both in and out of bed. Nell Gwyn did not like her and nor did the English people. It was not just that Louise was so obviously French, but that she was greedy for money and made sure she was

Louise de Kérouaille

kept well supplied with it. Louise's son with the king, another Charles, was made Duke of Richmond when he was 3 years old.

Louise was given various titles: Baroness Petersfield, Countess of Fareham and Duchess of Portsmouth. She also received the whacking great sum of £27,300. No wonder poor Nell was not pleased (though to be fair Charles did spend close to £60,000 on her over a three-year period).

Although Louise was Catholic she did not suffer the same fate as befell Barbara Palmer when the 1676 act was brought in preventing Catholics from holding any form of office within the royal household. This was because the queen intervened and had Louise made a member of her staff, who were exempt. Catherine, who had so hated Barbara Palmer, was more inclined to like Louise, who treated her with respect and was companionable. The queen may not have liked how her husband lived but she learned to put up with it as best she could.

Louise was with Charles when he died. She had been his constant companion throughout his illness and brought him solace at the end of his life, also insisting that he receive confession and absolution from a Catholic priest before he died.

After Charles's death Louise returned to France. England had not wanted her, did not like her, and James was not going to keep up her pension if he could help it. She did not live within her much diminished means and soon got into debt. Louis XIV and then the regent Philippe d'Orléans came to her rescue, bailed her out of her financial woes and settled a comfortable pension on her. She lived to be a venerable 85 years.

THE MISTRESSES OF GEORGE AUGUSTUS, PRINCE OF WALES

George IV

MARY 'PERDITA' ROBINSON (*NÉE* DARBY)

Mary Darby (1758–1800) was born into a comfortable and loving home. In her memoirs she describes it in great and affectionate detail. This cosy, safe world was suddenly whipped away from her when the family discovered why their father had been away so long in America: he had met someone else and wanted to set up home with her. The father whom Mary had known and adored was actually a selfish, heartless man, demanding the sale of the house that his legitimate family were living in.

Mary was not 10 years old at the time that her errant father called the family to London to meet with him so he could settle matters. She says in her memoirs that she was tall for her age and resembled a girl two or three years older. She was also very modest about her looks as a child, compared to those of her brothers.

The reunion with father and husband was painful on both sides. He hugged his children fervently and even gave his estranged wife a brief embrace. In her memoirs Mary tries hard not to lay the blame on him for the abandonment of his family, but rather to pin it on his new, young and scheming mistress.

His plans were to sell the house and everything in it and pay for bed and board for his wife in someone else's house. Mary and her brother (a younger boy, William, had died at the age of 6) were to attend school in London. Despite the trauma of being ripped from her home, Mary found school enlightening. She attributes all her learning to the inspiration provided by the schoolmistress, Meribah Lorrington, whom she describes as one of the most extraordinary women she had ever met.

The arrangement at the school was that Mary slept in the teacher's room at night, and this gave them the opportunity to continue lessons and conversations begun during the day. Out of the five or six students attending the school, Mary was by far the favourite, with her quick abilities and natural intelligence. Unfortunately Meribah Lorrington succumbed to only one vice, but it could paralyse her for days on end: she was an alcoholic. In one of their confidential after-school chats Mrs Lorrington confessed to Mary why she drank so heavily. She had lost her husband and had never got over it; she would

Mary 'Perdita' Robinson

try to numb the pain with drink. Many years later Mary encountered her old teacher in a very disturbing manner: an old crone came to the door asking for money and when Mary stared at her the woman asked if she didn't recognise her – it was Meribah Lorrington.

While Mary boarded at school her mother lived with a clergyman and his family nearby. Mary would visit them every Sunday and drink tea with her mother. On one of these visits Mary tells us that she was made an offer of marriage by a sea captain who was also a friend of her father's. He was absolutely astonished to hear that she was only 13, and had been sure she was at least three years older. He took his leave expressing hope that when he returned to London in two years' time, Mary might still be single. He was lost at sea a few months later. Mary suggests that England lost a gallant man; maybe she was thinking, wistfully, of what might have been.

Mrs Lorrington's school went broke about twelve months after Mary started there. She was sent to a boarding school in Battersea where she met another very talented teacher, Mrs Leigh. Although not as brilliant as Mrs Lorrington, she made up for the shortfall by not excessively indulging in alcohol. Mary says that she thinks she would have been happy at this establishment if her mother's own financial circumstances hadn't forced her to leave, as Mary's father had not been regular with his maintenance payments.

Mary's mother came up with a solution that she thought might benefit both of them: they would set up their own little boarding school in Chelsea and Mary would help teach classes; her special subject would be English. Within a short time, the school had about a dozen pupils. Just when it looked as though it would be a success Mary's father returned to London, furious at finding his wife and daughter earning money like common people. Mary defends him, talking of his pride, but the modern reader – and probably contemporary ones – would have decided he was an unreasonable hypocrite. To add insult to injury he took a house not far from where Mary's mother took lodging after he made her give up her school. He still kept them short of money and never visited them, although he would go walking with his daughter. He once confessed to Mary his regret at having taken up with the woman he now lived with, Eleanor, saying that life would have been so much easier if he hadn't have done. He was talking for himself, of course. Though he couldn't leave her, he told Mary, because he hadn't the funds to provide for her as well.

Mary completed her schooling at Oxford House just as she turned 15. The dancing master suggested she might think about making her living as an actress. By this time her father had again gone overseas (telling his wife that if anything bad happened to his daughter he would kill her). Even though Mary's mother nearly revoked her consent to her daughter becoming an actress, she finally agreed and the important introductions were made, the main one being to David Garrick. Mary would later recall how being in Garrick's company proved some of the best times of her life.

Even before she first made an appearance on stage, Mary was well in the public eye. She was to frequent the theatre as much as possible, according to the instructions of Mr Garrick. By doing this Mary found she was becoming the object of desire by various men, young and old, rich and poor, married and single. Mary's mother was almost beside herself keeping them away from her precious daughter.

Mary didn't have any inclinations towards any of these suitors until she was introduced to Mr Robinson. He was polite, attentive and kind. When her brother came down with smallpox he helped nurse him, assuring the family that he was there for them. Then Mary caught the disease and was very ill. Again Mr Robinson was there to support her mother. He was becoming indispensable to them. When Mary got better, her mother told her that she was to accept his hand in marriage.

Mary had little problem with this idea; Mr Robinson was good-looking and very amiable. The banns of marriage were published and the date for the wedding set, in April of her seventeenth year. And then, her beau asked her if they could keep the wedding a secret. He put forward a couple of reasons why they should do this, the first of which was understandable: Mr Robinson had not completed his articles with the firm of Messrs. Vernon and Elderton. The second reason, while understandable, was not wholly to Mary's liking and alarm bells went off. Apparently there was another young lady who was hoping he would ask her to marry him when the articles had expired.

Mary wanted to postpone the wedding but her fiancé was adamant they should marry sooner rather than later. Her mother also added pressure, thinking all the time of what her husband would do if he found out that she had let Mary go on the stage. The theatre manager wanted Mary to commit to an opening night and it was all too much pressure; Mary gave in to her mother and lover and got married without ever making her stage debut.

Once married Mary was to continue living with her mother until the couple could make their marriage public. This suited Mary, who tells us that she still enjoyed playing with her dolls at that time. Then the truth began to trickle out about the wonderful Mr Robinson. He still had ages to serve as a clerk; he was an illegitimate son of the man he claimed was his wealthy uncle and to whom he was heir. Yet the last was an outright lie: he was not expecting to inherit anything. Mary's mother was in despair. A trip to Wales followed in which Mr Robinson intended to prove he was the heir to his uncle's estate (a fact he kept insisting upon).

This story, given by Mary herself, differs from some of the others that have come to light. One of them states that Mary's mother found out the truth about Mr Robinson before the marriage and would have called it off but discovered that her daughter had already been seduced by the man and was in the family way. Another story says he had forged his papers to work as an articled clerk. Whether Mary didn't want the shocking truth revealed about having been seduced, or whether her own account is the real one, is a matter for debate.

In the end Mary was introduced to her husband's relative, Mr Harris, and made to feel almost but not quite welcome. She also met the formidable Miss Robinson, her husband's sister, who was not welcoming in the least. When the couple returned to London, openly as man and wife, things looked as though they might be all right. Until, that is, the odious Lord Lyttelton began to visit and cause trouble. He referred to Mary as 'the child' and would whisk her husband off to dens of iniquity. Lyttelton told Mary about Robinson's mistress, Harriet Wilmot, whom Mary confronted in the woman's own house. And by now Mary was pregnant.

The state of things declined from then on, and with creditors beginning to move in on them Robinson told Mary to get ready to go to Tregunter (his uncle's house in Wales). There was hope that Mr Harris might be able to tide things over for them. By this time Mary had also discovered that Robinson had other mistresses and that some of her precious belongings were being pilfered by him to be given as presents.

Mr Harris was extremely rude and told the pair that they had no business marrying without money, and that they should go and rot in jail. However, he did let Mary have her baby at his neighbouring house, Trevecca. It was comfortable and peaceful there and after the birth of her baby daughter, also called Mary, she was ecstatic. Mr Harris gave her barely time to recover from the birth before he packed her off. The little family went to spend time at Monmouth with Mary's grandmother.

The inevitable return to London had to be made, where Robinson was soon arrested and put into debtors' prison along with his faithful wife and their baby daughter. Mary consoled herself by writing poetry and, on contacting the Duchess of Devonshire, a young writer herself, managed to get a small volume of her poems published.

The family stayed in the debtors' prison for fifteen months. Mary would take leave to visit her new friend the duchess, but she found going back to her husband a trial, especially when she realised that he invited prostitutes in to entertain him while she was out. Finally they secured their freedom and moved into a modest dwelling. It was then that Mary bumped into an old acquaintance at the theatre and was inspired to try to earn her living there – as she had been planning to do before her marriage. Robinson was agreeable and Mary underwent an audition for Mr Sheridan. She was immediately engaged and her acting career took off.

Here again Mary's memoirs differ from most histories of Mrs Robinson. The common story is that her husband had abandoned her and helped himself to her earnings because, as her husband, he owned everything she had. Her own story is that they were still living as a couple and that, yes, he did spend too much of her money but it was with her own consent.

A trip to Wales followed in which Mr Robinson would prove he was the heir to his uncle's estate (and he kept insisting on it being that relationship):

Mr. Robinson, on his arrival at Tregunter, despatched a letter informing me that his 'uncle' seemed disposed to act handsomely, but that he had only ventured to avow an intention to marry, fearful of abruptly declaring that he had been already some months a husband. Mr. Harris, for that was the name of my father-in-law, replied that 'he hoped the object of his choice was not too young!' At this question Mr. Robinson was somewhat disconcerted.

They again visited Mr Harris in Wales, hoping that he might decide to be generous and bail his son out of debt. While not a penny was forthcoming, Mary's own welcome was a lot better than her previous one. Harris appreciated her efforts to earn money and congratulated her on it.

On their return to London Robinson was arrested yet again for debt, this time to a supposed friend of his, Mr Brereton. Brereton tried to blackmail Mary into becoming his mistress, saying he would let her husband off the charge if she did so. He told her he would await the pair of them in Bath so that she could pay her part of the bargain. Mary didn't tell her husband what had transpired, but when they got to Bath Mr Brereton was seen by them parading with his wife and her sister. Realising he was putting himself in a compromising position, Brereton let the matter drop and dismissed the debt.

Mary's acting career was blooming; she was becoming increasingly popular. Robinson began to despise her for it although he was always happy to spend her money. Soon Mary would take on the role of Perdita from Shakespeare's *A Winter's Tale*, the role in which the young Prince of Wales, later to be George IV, would first see her and fall in love with her.

Robinson begins to bow out of the story at this point. According to Mary's memoirs he is still living with her but is openly having affairs with women or visiting prostitutes.

The Prince of Wales saw Mary as Perdita and began to pursue her. They began an intense correspondence that lasted for four months before they actually spoke to one another. Mary writes about how she implored the prince to think hard about his passion for her, what the consequences for both of them would be, what his parents would think and how she could leave her husband.

These words of Mary's tend to make the reader think that she was trying hard to rectify a social mistake. She is too ardent in protecting the prince's interests and claiming that his attachment to her and his endearments were all given through real affection for her. She says it would be impossible for him to have been trying to 'trick her'. Mary ends her memoirs at the point when the prince is trying to get her to meet him at his apartments with her in disguise as a youth. Mary is adamant that she will not.

Perhaps Mrs Robinson was naive about the prince and his sincerity. Would she have given in to his demands if she had known that he and his gambling friends were having a wager on him getting her into bed?

Mary may have broken off telling her story at this point because of the deal she made with the royal family about her affair with the prince, which will emerge later in this story. To hear the end of the tale we must resort to the accounts of others. Some say that Mary got so sick of her husband's philandering ways that when she caught him with the maid, doing what he shouldn't, she finally threw him out; at least when she came to the decision to dine with the Prince of Wales she was no longer living with her husband. To attend her assignation Mary went in carnival costume, cloaked and masked. She dined not just with the prince but his younger brother, and told them her whole woeful history.

The prince decided the time was right for him to make her an offer that she would find hard to refuse. If she consented to live with him as his mistress then he would pay her the extraordinary sum of £100,000 (around £6 million today!). How Mary didn't get suspicious of such a large offer seems a bit odd but in the end she agreed to it. Further incentives may have clinched the deal. Mary was worried about her young daughter and her future. The prince would accommodate them, have her daughter educated and provide a good dowry for her on her marriage.

To her credit Mary insisted on the prince having a legal document drawn up with the payments and conditions as stated. He was to sign in front of witnesses. He tried to wriggle out of doing it and tried to threaten to kill himself if she didn't move in with him. She had wised up since she married and told him the deal was off unless she got the documents.

Thus, signed and sealed, Mrs Mary 'Perdita' Darby Robinson moved into luxury accommodation with her dashing young beaux, the Prince of Wales. Living as the prince's mistress did not seem to damage her reputation at all. It drew more crowds to see her at the theatre and she was always in demand for parties and other social events to which she might take the prince.

Underneath the surface of their beautiful relationship, and unbeknown to Mary, things were not all they seemed. She didn't realise that the prince was one of the worst gamblers in England; he played for high stakes and frequently lost. He would lose his temper and behave badly and he also had other women he was seeing besides Mary.

Mary decided to break her contract with the Drury Lane Theatre so that she could spend more time with the prince, who was claiming she never had enough time for him. Sheridan told her that if she did back out of her contract it would not be offered to her again. She nodded but continued to have it cancelled.

If only Mary had waited a while longer she would have discovered that her ardent lover was playing away from home and was on the point of dumping her entirely.

While she was out shopping for a party for the prince, the royal removalists moved into her apartment and packed up everything. When she returned she thought she'd been burgled. Neighbours told her what had happened and she traced her personal possessions to her husband's residence, but he was not going to let her have them back. The prince had terminated the lease on the flat (he always had his men put clauses into a lease so he could wriggle out when he wanted to). And, worst of all, Mary had just lost all chance of getting work on the stage to support herself. There was only one course of action and that was to go to the king, George III, to tell him what his son was capable of.

The king was more than aware of his eldest son's bad behaviour and, in his view, duping an actress – who he viewed as little better than a prostitute – paled into insignificance. For his part, the king was more worried about the enormous debts his son had accumulated through gambling. The signed document that Mary waved around as evidence of the prince's duplicity was nothing more than an irritation.

However, Mary had in her possession something far more damaging and which posed a real threat to the security of the monarchy: the prince's sexually explicit love letters to her. She wrote out a sample of some of the juiciest titbits and sent it along with her letter of complaint to the king. She was careful not to say anything that would suggest she was openly blackmailing the family, but it was inferred that if her demands were not met then the letters might happen to find their way into the hands of a journalist. And the public would have loved it.

Mary wanted the £25,000 that was only one-quarter of what she was originally promised. And if the prince's misdeeds weren't enough to scare His Majesty then Mary had another little scandal up her sleeve if necessary. Prince Frederick, the younger brother, had an illegitimate child with a common serving girl. The child had been placed with a decent family and Mary knew which one.

There was one big hurdle to Mary's plan, which was that the prince was already so in debt that his inheritance at 21, though still a little way off, was already spoken for. Lord Malvern, who was in love with Mary himself, tried to negotiate with her. In the end Mary settled for an immediate payment of £1,000 in exchange for a dozen of the letters. Later she would receive another amount for another dozen, and so forth. As she was desperate for money she felt she didn't have much option.

In order to squeeze more money out of the prince, Mary enlisted the help of Charles James Fox, a lawyer and politician. He too was attracted to Mary and tried to see what he could do. In the end, the best that could be got was an annual income of £500 plus £250 for Mary's daughter, to be paid to her annually for life. The letters were returned and destroyed. When George became king, still fearful of Mary's ability to damage his shaky reputation, she was also made to promise never to publish anything defamatory about him, which is probably why her memoirs end where they do. A small print-run of the memoirs was published after Mary's death and was made available only to close friends and family. It is now available as an e-book from www.gutenberg.org.

Mary had a brief fling with Fox, who was as cunning as his name. Although she quite enjoyed his witty company it was to the stalwart if rather dull Lord Malvern that she turned for further security. In return for a comfortable lifestyle and protection, Mary moved into his lavish London house and became his mistress. She made sure that her young child was kept close to her and was as amply provided for as Mary was herself.

Perhaps Mary would have spent the rest of her life as the privileged lover of Lord Malvern, but unfortunately she gave into temptation and spent a night of passion with Captain Banestre Tarleton, a friend of Malvern's. Mary's interest was aroused when she discovered Tarleton was an aspiring author, working on a history of the American War of Independence. This was the lure she could not resist. Her own ambition was to live by her writing, a most difficult thing to do in those times, especially for a woman. What she didn't know was that the charming captain had made a bet with his drinking friends that he could easily get into bed with her.

Mary gave her new lover two locks of hair, one from her head and one from her pubic area. Oddly, she didn't question that he asked for this (especially after the same thing had been requested so long ago by the Prince of Wales). They were, of course, trophies to be held aloft in the club where Lord Malvern became the butt of jokes; his beautiful mistress was nothing but a whore.

Mary got into her phaeton (one of the presents she had received from the prince) and raced off to find Malvern to see if the damage could be limited. On the way, the carriage crashed and Mary was pinned underneath it for more than an hour. It was Tarleton who came to her rescue. She was uninjured but in complete shock. Tarleton, to give him his due, was struck with remorse at having been the cause of such a nasty accident and drove her home to his own house. On settling and soothing her they discovered that they had a lot more in common than their one night stand.

Like so many men of his station, Tarleton was deep in debt and his family offered to pay off all his creditors if he took himself to France, without Mrs Robinson, and lived quietly for a while. Not seeing any other option Tarleton wrote to Mary explaining his situation but left without saying goodbye to her. Mary, anxious to keep hold of the man with whom she had so much to share, raised the funds to pay off his debts herself and chased after him to Dover to see if she could catch him before he embarked for France. Another pressing matter was the fact that she had discovered she was pregnant with his child.

The rough trip to Dover was too much for Mary, along with the anguish of losing yet another friend, and on the way she went into premature labour, losing the baby and then contracting rheumatic fever. She nearly died of it and was left very weak and permanently disabled afterwards. Tarleton returned as soon as he heard what had happened. When Mary was well enough the two of them went to live in France, where it was considerably cheaper to live comfortably.

Once across the Channel, Mary and Ban (the shortened form of his name) settled down to a life of writing. Mary helped Ban finish his manuscript of the war in America and then found a publisher for it. Mary herself kept writing poems and brought out a volume when the couple returned to London. Captain Tarleton became Colonel, although this did not help his financial situation, nor did his entering Parliament.

Mary was contented. She could not have any more children after her illness, which had also left her weak in the legs. Mary and Tarleton were together for fifteen companionable years. And then Tarleton did a most astonishing and underhand thing: he married a young woman who would give him an heir. It was done to please his parents but he neglected to tell Mary; she learned of his engagement through the newspaper.

It was the ultimate betrayal: worse than her father's, worse than her husband's, much worse than the prince's – this was the end of her relationships with men. She wrote a novel *The False Friend*. In it she warned young women to beware of the romantic suitor. The book became a success and a second edition was published. Sales rocketed when it became known that the author was none other than Perdita Robinson who had been a stage sensation and mistress to the Prince of Wales.

Mary 'Perdita' Darby Robinson died in 1800.

MARIA FITZHERBERT (*NÉE* SMYTHE)

The woman who kept a prince

George IV kept up the family tradition of having a stack of women at his disposal. Some of them were no more than prostitutes, paid in cash for their services, others were longer-term arrangements. George and his brothers began this habit while they were all still in their teens; between them they fathered numerous illegitimate offspring.

This is the story of a woman who was particularly hard to get into bed and had to be tricked into what she thought was a legitimate marriage before she would sleep with him.

Maria Smythe (1756–1837) was a convent-educated girl from a good Catholic family. Catholicism was a difficult religion to practise in England towards the end of the eighteenth century. It was not illegal but there were no public Catholic services to attend and all marriages had to be performed as Anglican ones first or they were deemed illegal.

When she was 18 Maria fell in love with a handsome young man who had an estate and promised to look after her. His name was Edward Weld. The two underwent the obligatory first Anglican wedding and finished with a private Catholic service at her own home. All was set for a perfect life.

Not three months after the wedding took place, Edward was thrown from his horse and seriously injured. Maria, although distraught, nursed her husband until he died shortly after. Unfortunately, there had been an oversight. Because of their youth and the fact they hadn't been married very long, Edward had forgotten to make provision for his wife in his will. He should have followed the normal procedure of fixing a percentage of his estate and fortune on Maria so she could live comfortably after his death. Instead everything went to Edward's younger brother, who refused to give his sister-in-law anything.

In such a case there was only one viable option for a young woman and that was to return to her father's house. Not long before she got there he had suffered a heart attack and it had left him partially paralysed. Maria was happy to tend her father and live a quiet life to mourn her husband.

Maria Fitzherbert

It was not to be. Maria's aunt, Lady Isabella Sefton, decided it was not a healthy proposition for such an attractive young widow and dragged Maria out of her retirement to spend four months of the social season with her in town. Isabella had only her niece's welfare in mind; although Maria didn't have a dowry Isabella felt certain they would be able to find someone suitable for her.

The Earl of Sefton already had someone in mind, Thomas Fitzherbert: a widower, a Catholic, wealthy and of good reputation. He was ten years older than Maria. Fitzherbert came to dinner, sat next to Maria and found her quite delightful but also without affected airs. She was natural, sweet and modest. He asked the earl if he could pay his attentions to her.

They married on 24 June 1778, again with two ceremonies. Maria was 22. The first ceremony was conducted in public in the village church and then the Catholic one was held in Fitzherbert's private chapel on his estate, Swynnerton Hall. It was another love match of two mature and quiet people. Within six months they were expecting a baby. Then Maria had a miscarriage. She went into a decline and her husband worried about her health. He decided she needed a change of scene and swept her off to London.

A popular activity amongst the wealthy socialites of London was to drive in a carriage through Hyde Park, particularly the south side's Rotten Row (at the end of the eighteenth century this was a wide pathway some 4,541 feet long). Fitzherbert took his grieving wife for an afternoon to Rotten Row. Before long the couple became aware of a young man on horseback riding alongside them and staring very rudely at her. She ignored him. Later, her husband informed her that her admirer was the Prince of Wales and that he had a dreadful reputation as a womaniser and made no discrimination between married and unmarried. Maria was put on her guard. Her aunt also reinforced the warnings when she was told of the incident. The Prince of Wales was not a good man, even though he was heir to the throne of England.

In 1778 the Papists Act was passed in Parliament in an attempt to stem the intolerance towards the Catholic community. The act upset a lot of people and, just as Fitzherbert feared, there were public outbursts of anger and violence. It culminated in a series of riots in which the homes and businesses of Catholics were set fire to. One evening Maria's brother-in-law came to their house in London in a terrible state, calling on her husband to come and help quell the fires and save people's homes and lives. Ever ready to help, Fitzherbert rushed out into the night.

He returned in the morning, covered in ash, soot, black, burned and exhausted. Maria put him straight to bed, already fearing the worst. Within hours she had a doctor to see him, he was desperately ill. He was suffering from severe smoke inhalation. The doctor advised a change of climate as soon as possible, perhaps to the south of France.

Maria would have done anything to help her beloved husband recover, and having spent years at school in France she was more than proficient in the language. They settled in Nice. Thomas Fitzherbert knew he wouldn't ever get better, he found it hard to breathe and was wracked with pain. He arranged for his London lawyer to visit him in Nice. Fitzherbert made sure Maria would be left very comfortable after he was gone. The bulk of the estate would pass to a younger brother, this was the usual way of things, but a nice amount was put aside for Maria.

At the age of 37 the heroic Fitzherbert died in the arms of his wife. She couldn't get his body back to England so had to have him buried in France. As soon as she could, Maria took herself back to the convent where she had been educated, to be cared for by the kind nuns she knew so well. She longed for solitude. She had lost two husbands, both of whom she had loved and had been loved by. There were no children from either marriage to bring comfort to her.

It is highly likely that Maria would have stayed in France, but the French Revolution was looming and she was urged to go home to England as soon as she could. In 1783 she returned home only to find her pending arrival had been splashed across the society pages of the newspapers. It was the last thing she wanted.

Following this there were further newspaper items about the young, attractive widow and her fortune, speculating on who would be the first to woo her. All Maria wanted to do was to be left alone to grieve. Her aunt had other ideas, not to see her remarried necessarily, but she didn't think it a good thing for her niece to be so wrapped up in her sorrow. They went to Covent Garden to the opera, sitting in a private box where Maria could watch without being gazed upon by a curious public, or so she thought. However, a pair of opera glasses was trained her way and the Prince of Wales spent the whole evening watching the beautiful young woman he had stared at in the park all those years before.

In the general bustle of leaving the theatre, the prince asked Maria's uncle to introduce them. It was done unwillingly as the earl knew what the prince was up to. Maria for her part did not like the pushy young man.

The prince found Maria's reluctance to see him very enticing. He was working himself up into a fixation with her. He enlisted the help of his dear friend Georgiana, Duchess of Devonshire (and whose own story appears in this volume). Georgiana didn't think much of the prince's choice for his latest paramour but she agreed to hold a luncheon party and invite the widow – and to sit her next to the prince.

At the lunch Maria ignored her admirer as much as she could without being openly rude. She was heeding her friends' warnings about him and alarm bells were ringing loudly. On her return home Maria's aunt again warned her about the Prince's reputation. The warning was hammered home when later that day a large bunch of flowers and a bracelet were delivered to Maria at her aunt's house. She kept the flowers and sent a note thanking the prince for them, but returned the bracelet saying she couldn't accept that kind of gift.

The prince was far from discouraged and made sure Maria was invited to more gatherings so that they could be thrown together. Despite herself Maria enjoyed the social activities; she even began to enjoy the prince's company. He was an art lover, particularly of French art and this was one of Maria's own passions. As their friendship grew, the prince sent her a miniature of himself set in a locket. Maria did not feel the need to send back this item of jewellery and she wore it often. Had she known it was almost identical, although smaller, to one that the prince had given to Perdita Robinson, she may have thought differently.

Maria told her priest of her growing fondness for the prince. He advised her to live a quieter life and move to the country, making accessibility to her more difficult. She took the advice but didn't move far enough away. She settled on a house in Richmond and began to restore the gardens there. It was not more than a carriage ride, and no distance at all on horseback, so the prince was easily able to visit her in her country idyll. Maria continued to reject his now quite open declarations of love.

Rumours began to issue forth that the prince was so in love with the young widow that he was going to propose marriage. Whether he had any real intention of doing so had no bearing on the matter. He was not yet 25 and therefore could not marry anyone without his father's (the king's) permission. What is more, he could not legally marry a Catholic and keep his claim to the throne of England. There was huge opposition to having a Catholic monarch ruling in England. If he had married Maria without his father's consent then the marriage could be declared null and void. Maria knew this and so did the prince. Yet it seems that the prince was a young man totally self-absorbed. It is doubtful whether he thought further than his immediate pleasure and if he could get Maria into bed he would marry her without thought of the consequences.

Maria, afraid of more rumours circulating to damage her reputation, took on a companion, an older woman, to act as chaperone for the prince's visits. This meant Maria could begin to really enjoy the prince's company. Instead of taking it slowly and steadily the prince began to pressure Maria with his assertions, that he needed her to help compensate for his lonely childhood. She sympathised but, wisely, would not give in.

Maria's confessor advised her to go away again; France was his suggestion. She would go back to her convent and be safe. She told the prince that she did love him but that as they could never be married it was best for her to remove herself from temptation and leave him to fall in love with someone else. The prince's response was to threaten to kill himself. In July 1784 he pierced his chest with an ornamental dagger, just enough to draw blood. He ordered his barber to dress the wound with used bandages so that the damage would look greater. He then sent a message to Maria that he was dying of a self-inflicted wound. She was horrified, worried but suspicious too. Her chaperone wasn't available to go with her to see the prince so in desperation she called on the Duchess of Devonshire to go with her.

The scene of the prince, pale and lying still on a bed swathed in bloodied bandages, was enough to make Maria swoon, even if she hadn't already nursed two husbands as they were dying. Yet surely she must have realised it was nothing more than a ruse to get her to do his bidding? Although trying not to judge her, one has to wonder why she wasn't furiously indignant that he dared to pretend he was dying when both her husbands, who had been good men, had suffered real fatal injuries.

Perhaps Maria was so truly in love with the prince that she was prepared to be duped. As she was about to leave the prince swore his love for her and promised he would marry her, giving his word on the ring he kissed and placed on her finger (and which he had to ask the Duchess of Devonshire for). Maria took her leave. As she was getting into her carriage Lord Southampton ran after her saying she was to sign a document to the effect that she would marry the prince. The duchess took her to Devonshire House where the paperwork was prepared and signed by Maria before witnesses. Tired, distraught and not thinking properly, Maria Fitzherbert had unwittingly signed the document that would seal her fate.

On returning home to finish packing, and thinking hard upon what had happened, Maria realised she had been tricked. If the document got into the hands of the king she could be arrested. It was illegal to enter into an agreement to marry the prince without the king's permission and she would be seen to be as guilty as the prince. He would be admonished but she could serve a prison sentence.

France and the convent seemed safer and more attractive than ever. Maria finished her packing and took off without leaving a clue as to where she was going. The prince pleaded with his father to let him go after her but, of course, the request was refused. The king was anxious for the nonsense to be over and once again told his son it was time he married a suitable Protestant princess. It fell on deaf ears. The king changed tactic and promised to pay off his son's outrageous gambling debts, as well as give him money to help with his extensive renovations of the prince's residence at Carlton House. Money talked and the prince agreed to settle down, yet he did not take any steps towards fulfilling his promise.

Instead of searching for a suitable wife the prince sent his friend, the Duke d'Orléans to track down the missing Maria. When her place of hiding was discovered the prince bombarded her with passionate letters imploring her to return to him.

Finally, worn down by his entreaties and wanting to go home, Maria decided she might be able to undergo a morganatic marriage with the prince. This would mean that any children from the union would be legitimate but would not be able to inherit from their father, and therefore not pose a threat to the throne. She asked her priest whether such a secret marriage would be recognised by her Church and was assured that it would, although it would be considered illegal by the law of England.

In December 1785 Maria returned to England and married the Prince of Wales in a secret ceremony held in her own house, with her uncle and brother as witnesses. The clergyman who married them was easily persuaded to do so. He asked a fee of £500, and to be appointed as one of the prince's chaplains, to be upgraded to that of bishop when the prince ascended the throne.

The happy couple honeymooned at Richmond. Although the affair was kept very secret, something was leaked to the press and again the papers were rife with speculation. Maria was most afraid of being labelled the prince's mistress, although she didn't want to be put into prison either. She sent queries to Cardinal Weld, the Pope's emissary, as to whether or not what she had done constituted a proper marriage in the eyes of God. The answer was affirmative.

When things got difficult for the prince in Parliament, Maria, faithful to her husband, hid all documentary evidence of the marriage. She removed the signatures of her relatives so there would be no recriminations against them and had the marriage certificate buried in the vault of her bank. The crisis was removed but in the process Maria found that her lover was not prepared to declare his marriage to her openly for fear of being disinherited. Maria went along with it so that he would not be ruined but she was very hurt by his actions and refused to have anything to do with him for two months.

Because she sincerely loved the prince, he was able to worm his way back into Maria's affections. She knew they were married but she let herself be publicly acknowledged as his mistress; in 1786 they moved to Brighton where it was hoped they could live more economically and reduce some of the prince's debts. Even though the prince's debts had been paid off after his promise to his father to make a politically correct marriage, they had mounted up again. The prince had magnanimously allocated an entertainment allowance to Maria so that she could preside over dinners and gatherings for him and his friends. It was little more than a gesture and ended with Maria having to pay for it all herself. She rented a house in Brighton that was to be her official residence, while the prince bought himself a rundown old farmhouse on which he would spend huge amounts of money doing it up.

Although Maria had to pay for her own upkeep and for entertaining the prince's friends, the time she spent in Brighton with her husband was some of the happiest. They went bathing in the sea out of the bathing machines, little wooden huts on wheels that were drawn into the surf by horses. Steps at the back went down into the water and men and women could immerse themselves in the water in private. They went for walks, had dinner parties and were able to enjoy each other's company more or less without restriction. It was noticed that the prince was in better health and that he had lessened his gambling and drinking. Maria was so entranced by Brighton that she had a house built there.

Like all things, good ones come to an end too. They both returned to London. The prince had official business to attend to and Maria had a house in the city to maintain. While back in London the prince dined with his parents; the king suddenly got up in the middle of dinner, went around to his son and began attacking him. He tried to throttle him with his bare hands. After being subdued by his attendants the king was then put to bed. It appeared to everyone that the king might be losing his sanity and that the prince would have to step in as regent. Yet it wasn't quite the time for that, the king got better and was able to resume business as usual. Maria returned to Brighton, followed soon after by the prince.

It was a tumultuous time. The French had executed their royal house and French aristocrats were seeking refuge in England. Many of them brought jewellery and heirlooms with them to be converted into cash. The prince was in his element buying up French artworks and getting further and further into debt yet again. England was preparing for war with France and was not able to overlook the prince's extravagant ways. The king issued an ultimatum to his son: marry one of two German Protestant princesses, both of whom were his cousins, or else.

Lady Jersey, one of the queen's ladies-in-waiting, at her mistress's command made the choice for him. Caroline of Brunswick was chosen. She was said to have been averse to washing regularly, was overly plump and not at all pretty. The prince needed to be prised away from his darling Maria, so the same Lady Jersey could use her seductive ways to lure him into her own bed. The prince had had other lovers besides Maria all through their relationship so this was nothing new.

With the prince under the thumb of Lady Jersey he was persuaded, again for large sums of money, to give up Maria altogether and marry his cousin. The prince sent Maria a letter informing her of his intended marriage and that it meant he would never see her again. To say that Maria was stunned and heartbroken would be an understatement, although she probably knew deep down that it was bound to happen.

The prince met his bride-to-be not long before the wedding day. Neither party was impressed. The prince, always fastidious about personal hygiene, was genuinely revolted by Caroline's lack of it; on her part, she told one of her gentlemen in attendance that the Prince was fat and not as handsome as he was supposed to be.

On the morning of the wedding the Prince sent a love letter to Maria, but she was unimpressed and ignored it. The wedding was endured by all and the marriage consummated (at least it was thought to have been because nine months later baby Charlotte was born). The Prince was in a terrible state and drowned his sorrows regularly. In one such drunken fit he wrote a note leaving everything he owned to Maria, which probably in truth amounted to a huge debt.

Maria, as in the past, took the Prince back into her life, but determined that she would be the boss this time. It was to be a platonic relationship only. Maria, although she loved him, still held her Catholic beliefs above all else. She had by this time received a direct missive from the Pope assuring her of the validity of her marriage to the Prince. The marriage between him and Caroline had been a total disaster from the start and once she had produced an heir for him then she was nothing more than a nuisance. Caroline had a mind of her own and was not afraid to use it. She had already got rid of the nauseating Lady Jersey who had done nothing but try to stir up trouble for her. Although by law the couple could not divorce, Caroline was finally paid off to go and live in Italy, which she did quite happily.

The Prince, sulky because Maria would no longer sleep with him, turned his attentions to someone else. Lady Isabella Herford was his choice; or rather she engineered it to be his choice. Maria was furious and extremely jealous. The last straw came at a dinner given by the Prince. Unusually Maria was not asked to arrange it, although she was invited to it. When she got there she found her place beside the Prince had been usurped by Lady Herford who was openly flirting and playing with the Prince, feeding him from her fork – and he was revelling in it. Maria, absolutely disgusted, got up from the table and walked out. She would never see her Prince again.

Maria settled down in her house in Brighton and lived there until her death in 1837. She was loved by the population there, as she had been instrumental in turning around the economics of the town. It had been poor and shabby, nothing more than a fishing village until she and the Prince took notice of it. It became a busy and prosperous place where the wealthy came to take the invigorating sea air and to bathe in the cold ocean waters. It never looked back.

EDWARD DAVID

(EDWARD VIII, PRINCE OF WALES) — BEFORE WALLIS

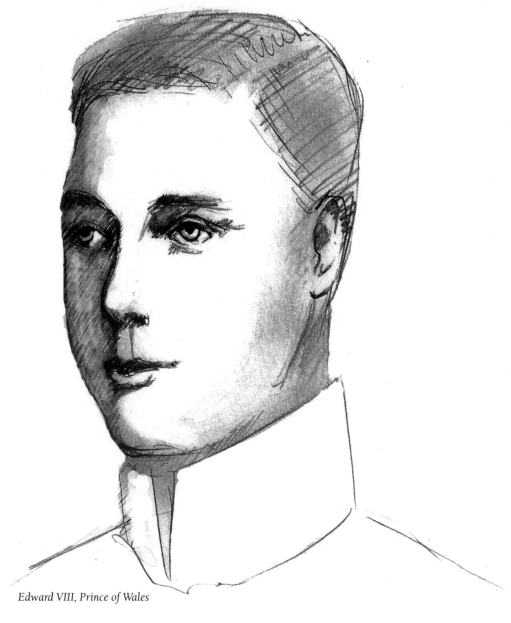

Edward VIII, Prince of Wales

FREDA DUDLEY WARD (*NÉE* BIRKIN)

We all know the outcome of the famous love affair between Edward David, the Prince of Wales (Edward VIII), and the infamously divorced Wallis Simpson. Because it caused such a scandal, resulting in the abdication of the king, perhaps it has overshadowed some of the prince's earlier affairs. One of the first of these serious liaisons was with a married woman, Freda (Winifred) Dudley Ward (*née* Birkin).

Winifred Birkin (1891–1983)was born into a well-to-do family. Her father, a colonel, owned a lace manufacturing business. His daughter had been given independence through a generous allowance, which meant that she was able to sustain a lavish lifestyle. When she was 18 she had married William Dudley Ward, age 34. Within the next five years their two girls were born. Ward was establishing his political career, which may have been one of the reasons that the couple decided not to divorce.

So, Freda was 23 and a mother of two daughters when she first met Prince Edward. They met entirely by accident during an air raid in February 1918. Freda was married but she and her husband, having realised they were not compatible, had settled on an amicable solution where they lived quite separate lives. Freda had money and domestic staff to run her home and look after her children when she felt like socialising. After the marriage failed, she had not been slow to begin enjoying herself again; she had already had a couple of minor affairs.

On the night she met the prince, Freda had been out dancing with a young man, Beau Dominguez. They were strolling through the streets when the air-raid siren went off. They immediately looked for shelter and rushed over to a nearby house. By chance it belonged to Mrs Maude Kerr-Smiley, who also just happened to be the older sister of Ernest Simpson. Although Wallis was not yet on the scene, she was already making an appearance; Ernest was her first husband.

Mrs Kerr-Smiley ushered them into the house and straight down the stairs to the cellar where her own guests were sheltering until the German airships had gone. Freda and her beau soon realised the company they were in and Freda took no time in placing herself next to Edward. The two chatted away very cheerfully after their initial

Freda Dudley Ward

introduction and it turned out that they had a lot in common. They parted, each keen to see the other again soon.

Friendship gave way to an affair without much delay. The prince took to Freda's domestic situation with great enthusiasm. He played with the girls, had picnics and let Freda treat him as if he were just one of the children. Edward wrote to her frequently and the two of them had pet names for each other. Freda, however, knew of her position. It is likely that she had never wanted to be his wife but she knew it was impossible anyway, as he would have to renounce his claim to the throne if he married a divorcée, which she wasn't anyway – she was still married.

After the war Edward was forced to go on a tour of Canada, followed by America. In Alberta he bought a ranch with some expectation of discovering oil on it. He wrote to Freda telling her that all he wanted was to live there with her. Of course it was pure fantasy, they both knew that. Throughout the tour the prince wrote constantly to his lover, not only telling her of his daily doings but always declaring his passion for her and how much he missed her. More than 260 letters from Edward to Freda were discovered in the 1980s by a stamp collector. When they came to auction they realised an enormous sum. The letters are very revealing of the nature of the affair and how the prince referred to Freda as 'Little Mummy' and he was her 'Little David'. Correspondence from Freda to the prince has not come to light, probably having been destroyed.

If Edward thought his time in Canada was too long to be away from Freda then his trip to Australia and New Zealand the following year was even worse. His letters complain of his position and how he detested it; visiting numerous institutions and greeting hordes of people was something he thought he would never get used to or enjoy.

What did Freda think of it all? How did she cope with her lover being away for so long and so often? Apparently she was already tiring of the affair and on the lookout for someone less dependent on her. Over the next few months she gradually weaned him off her. Their sexual relationship ended, much to the relief of the prince's relatives. Freda maintained a steady friendship with Edward for years later, acting as his confidante and adviser in romantic issues.

After his affair with Freda Ward, the prince met Thelma Furness, whose story will be told after this one. Freda stayed in contact with Edward all the time he was seeing Thelma and there was never a problem between the two women. Then, in the early 1930s, Freda suddenly found that she was no longer able to contact him. Her calls, she was told abruptly, would not be accepted. And that was the end of the relationship entirely.

Freda lived to the ripe old age of 92; she died in 1983. When her family cleared out her house, 313 love letters were found from Edward, Prince of Wales, to Freda Dudley Ward. They were very intimate and revealed much about the prince. Freda must have answered at least some of them but no trace of these has been found. Speculation is that they either belong in the royal archives or were destroyed as embarrassing evidence – or that Mrs Wallis Simpson did away with them through jealousy.

LADY THELMA MORGAN FURNESS

Exit Freda Ward, enter Thelma Hays Morgan (1905–70). Thelma and her identical twin, Gloria, were born to an American father and a Chilean mother and were two of four children. Harry Hays Morgan was a diplomat and had postings all around the world. The twins were actually born in Switzerland when he was posted as American consul there. The children all spoke Spanish as their first language and English, or rather, American, as their close second. The three girls were brought up by nannies and governesses; Harry, the only boy, was sent to boarding school as soon as he was old enough. As part of a lady's upbringing at the time it was still considered appropriate for the girls to learn how to dance, sing, draw and write elegant letters. Consuelo, the elder of the three sisters was also a bookworm, while the twins were not. All the children were multilingual.

When the siblings grew up Harry went straight to Hollywood; Consuelo was forced into an arranged marriage with a man who turned out to be a trickster and which ended in a very quick annulment; the twins were convent educated and excelled in dress design and sewing. Consuelo quickly found a suitable husband for herself in a young American diplomat. In the meantime, the twins would stay at a finishing school, preparing for a sensational debut into society. Finishing school was not what the girls had in mind for themselves at all and they contacted their father for help. He gave them an allowance between them so that they could live independently in a flat in New York.

At the age of 16 the twins decked themselves out in stunning dresses of their own design and began telling people they were older than they were in order to get invited to parties, hoping to find suitable husbands rather than be forced into some dreadful relationship by their mother. Unfortunately Thelma fell into the same kind of trap as her older sister, only unlike Consuelo, Thelma had only herself to blame. James Vail Converse was indeed who he claimed to be, part of the wealthy Bell telephone clan. What he was not was an independent, hard-working member of that family. He'd gambled and drunk his inheritance away and was on the lookout for a wife with lots of money.

Thelma's marriage to him was a disaster. Her sister Gloria also chose a man of her own. Another wealthy family with another spendthrift son: Reggie Vanderbilt. He had been married and divorced before and had two children whom he had provided for by putting money in a trust fund for them. Reggie's mother, aware of her son's position financially and his spending habits, gave the couple an allowance that would keep them very comfortably. Reggie was more than twice Gloria's age, had been a heavy drinker and had a seriously damaged liver.

Apart from these trifles Gloria's marriage turned out to be relatively happy and their daughter, Gloria Laura, was born in 1924. She too would inherit from the trust fund when her father died. Alice Vanderbilt bought her son and daughter-in-law a beautiful house in New York in which they could entertain and bring up the children in the way Vanderbilt children were supposed to be, very wealthy.

Thelma was able to divorce her husband with the help of her two sisters. She then went to live with Harry in Hollywood, where he had not managed to make his fortune. Thelma, always a promising dancer – in fact she had wanted to be a professional dancer from childhood – found work alongside Mary Pickford, though it did not

Lady Thelma Morgan Furness

seem to get her any further in her aspirations to be a movie star. She received a divorce settlement of US$100,000 (around $1 million today) when she came of age and used it to set up her own film production company, probably inspired by the one Mary Pickford and her husband Douglas Fairbanks had started. As head of her own production company Thelma could choose her own stars – and she chose herself. Co-stars included the well-known Clara Bow and Lionel Barrymore, amongst others. If she had persevered with the company and taken on new technology, gone into talkies, then maybe Thelma could have made a name in cinema. But she let her mother talk her out of it; she sold up and went to live with her sister in New York. It was there, at one of their many dinner parties, that Thelma met her second husband, Lord Marmaduke Furness, a widower. He was wealthy and an aristocrat, charming but also boring; his favourite hobbies were fox hunting and riding. Thelma detested horses: it should have been a warning to her.

By their third date he had proposed and she had accepted. To be fair, though, Thelma did get a taste of what life with Furness would be like, as they began a sexual relationship as fiancées. They were married at a registry office in London in 1926 with only a few guests, two of whom were Consuelo and her husband Bernie.

Furness was away on business much of the time and he gave his wife a sports car so she could go gadding about the countryside. Then the truth about the fabulous, generous husband began to emerge. He was an alcoholic who got violent; he wouldn't let Thelma have an allowance of her own, although she was allowed to buy lots of clothes and finery as long as it was charged to his account. And, worst of all, he hated children. He hated his own two from his first marriage in particular. His son tried to have as little to do with his family as possible and was at Eton most of the year. Averill, by the time she was 18 – and not very attractive – was the butt of her father's cruel taunts. Both Thelma and Averill were in trouble when Averill's debut into society failed to produce her a suitor. And to add another thing to his list of grievances against Thelma, she had not yet got pregnant.

Enter the Prince of Wales. He and Thelma met at a ball in 1926. Thelma hadn't been long married to Furness. Edward found Thelma exotic and glamorous having come from Hollywood. He invited her and her husband to a jazz concert but Furness declined because of business commitments; Thelma later found that a ticket had been sent to her London address – and she went.

They drank champagne, talked and danced, drank more champagne, confided in each other and then went to bed together in a hotel. The next step was a weekend in the country. From then on Thelma would spend as much time as possible with her royal lover, which meant any time her husband was away.

In 1928 the Furnesses were set to go on an African safari, it was business for the husband and supposedly pleasure for his wife. The Prince of Wales was able to comfort Thelma with the promise that he would be in Africa at the same time, also on safari. He would send them an invitation to join his travelling party. Once again Furness declined the offer but was only too willing for his wife to go, where she could make useful contacts. Thelma enjoyed herself immensely while travelling with her lover, the only blight being the possibility she may be pregnant and would not know who the father was, her husband or her lover.

Furness was delighted to hear the news that his wife was expecting a baby, and she had a story readily prepared in order to explain any colouring the child might exhibit at birth – neither Furness nor Thelma were fair haired or blue eyed. Thelma did actually have some Irish ancestry and she would use that as the reason, although she had given nothing away that might let Furness suspect she had been unfaithful. The baby was a boy, much to his father's delight – although he did not take any other interest in him – and he had dark hair like his mother.

Thelma's life went along in a comfortable way. Her husband was frequently out of the country on business (or more likely gambling), she had her prince to keep her happy and her beloved older sister Consuelo, she had a darling baby boy and lived in luxury. Then something happened that was to ruin everything.

Enter Mrs Wallis Simpson. After having been introduced to Thelma by her sister, Thelma invited the Simpsons to a dinner party she was giving in honour of the prince's return from an overseas trip. Nothing of any significance happened at the dinner – that was to come later.

It was Maria Dudley Ward who had met Mrs Kerr-Smiley towards the end of the war when she took shelter in her house during an air raid: Maria had met the prince there and become his mistress, then his dear friend in whom he often confided. Now here was Mrs Kerr-Smiley's sister-in-law Wallis wanting Thelma to help her get an introduction at court. Thelma didn't know it but Maude Kerr-Smiley did not like Wallis, did not trust her and thought she was just after her brother's money. She was not going to introduce her at court. Thelma arranged for an acquaintance of her husband, who had performed the same service for her, to do it in return for a cash payment.

Thelma attended the presentation and the evening ended with a congenial supper at her own house for the Simpsons and the prince. The meal was reciprocated by a dinner at the Simpsons'. The friendship grew between Wallis and Thelma, and Wallis and the prince. The two women would spend time at the prince's estate, Thelma feeling safe in the knowledge that if Furness were to get curious he would find his wife had a worthy chaperone and that the two of them were overseeing young women being presented as potential wives to the prince. Furness was busy having an affair of his own anyway, so was probably too wrapped up in his other woman to notice.

Thelma's marriage finally ended in divorce. She had discovered her husband's other woman and he in turn had accused her of having an affair with the Prince of Wales, although she denied it. He threatened to divorce her on those grounds. Her lawyers suggested she put forward the proceedings for divorce first and get an affidavit from an employee of Furness's mistress to say she had seen the two in bed together. When Furness told his lawyers he'd push his claim through, they told him very decisively that he would be mad to involve the prince in any way.

When the divorce came through there was little money for Thelma and she lost custody of their son. Furness married his mistress as quickly as possible. The two young children from the mistress's previous marriage, and Anthony, were looked after in a separate wing of the great house Furness owned and looked after by a series of nannies.

Thelma's life took a downturn from then on. She was free to see the prince although she knew she could never be married to him, her son was banished from her and she had no money. To top it all,

Wallis Simpson was becoming increasingly attractive to the Prince of Wales.

At the same time that Thelma was losing custody of her son, Gloria was battling for custody of her daughter. Gloria's husband had died and his sister Gertrude Vanderbilt was trying to get hold of her brother's little daughter. Gloria begged Thelma to help her through the emotional turmoil. Thelma obliged and set off for New York, promising the prince she would see him again as soon as she could.

While in America Thelma met a very handsome man, Prince Aly Khan, with whom a casual dance led to a brief fling. On her return to London Thelma found that photos of her with the prince had made it into the hands of Wallis Simpson, who had shown them to Edward with the purpose of turning him from his mistress. When Thelma asked to visit him Edward suggested they have a break from each other. Thelma drove to the prince's estate only to find that her place at his side had been well and truly usurped by Wallis Simpson. And that was the end of the affair between Thelma Furness and Edward David, the Prince of Wales.

Thelma embarked on a relationship with Prince Aly Khan, although she knew it was no more than an extended fling. Finally, after a huge battle with Furness's third wife over Anthony's inheritance, Thelma returned to Hollywood to live with her widowed twin sister. She died in 1970 in New York.

Part 3
Mistresses of the Aristocracy

THE MISTRESSES OF THE DUKE OF DEVONSHIRE

William Cavendish became the 5th Duke of Devonshire when he was age 16. His father had died a rather embittered man, dismissed from his post as Lord Chamberlain by George III because of his leadership of the Whig party. The young king subsequently assembled his own government; one he thought he could trust.

William, on becoming Duke of Devonshire, was automatically catapulted into the middle of Whig politics; a position for which he had neither the interest nor the talent. It was remarked by some of his colleagues in the party that, although he looked the part, he did not have the aptitude and was well known for his indifference. The same indifference seems to have spread to the feelings he had for his first wife, Georgiana Spencer. Various sources suggest that he was a man who liked his women particularly attentive to his comfort, who pandered to his whims and who did not make great public waves, as she tended to do.

Whatever the secret to his charm, twice during his lifetime the duke had both a wife and mistress – the same wife but a different mistress. The second mistress was taken into the bosom of his family and became indispensable to both husband and wife in a genuine ménage a trois.

The three women presented here have stories that intertwine so it seems best to tell their stories together: Georgiana Cavendish, the Duchess of Devonshire (b.1757; d.1806); Charlotte Spencer (d.1778); Lady Elizabeth Hervey Foster (later Duchess of Devonshire) (b.1759; d.1824).

Georgiana was a beautiful, intelligent young woman who earned a reputation for being both a leader of fashion and a notorious gambler. Her life with her husband and his mistresses is a fascinating one.

Georgiana's father was John Spencer, 1st Earl Spencer; her mother was Lady Margaret Spencer (*née* Poyntz). Georgiana, the eldest child of three, was her mother's favourite and the two declared themselves best friends. Poor little Harriet who came along five years later was not so lucky, her mother pronounced her as an ugly baby and left it at that.

When she was 16 Georgiana was introduced to the 24-year-old Duke of Devonshire. After a brief interlude, in which the two young people were thrown together socially, the duke put forward his request to marry Georgiana. The offer was accepted and the date of the wedding set for Georgiana's seventeenth birthday. The match was considered a very good one. The Spencers and the Devonshires were socially on a par and Georgiana was going to have a splendid dowry settled on her at marriage; the duke was good-looking and charming.

Georgiana's wedding was an expensive affair. Her family spent a lot of money setting her up with wedding clothes and jewels, post-wedding clothes such as walking dresses, ball gowns, morning dresses, riding habits, stockings, gloves, hats, shoes (reportedly sixty-five pairs) and anything else that would help make her happy in her new home and enhance her beauty as a showpiece for her husband. Even though a lot of time and money went into the preparations, only five people actually attended the wedding itself.

What more could a 17-year-old girl want? One thing she certainly did not want was a rival for her new husband's affections. Charlotte

Spencer – and no, she was not related to Georgiana's family – already had a strong hold on the duke's heart.

Charlotte had been destined to become a milliner in London. Her father was a clergyman with a poor living who died when she was a teenager. Although she could have made a go of it in the city, her life took an abrupt turn for the worse almost as soon as she stepped off the coach. A common practice in those days was for parasitic men to introduce themselves to young country girls as they alighted in London. They offered to help them find accommodation and work or offered them love and marriage; the results were usually disastrous. Seduced and abandoned Charlotte found refuge with a wealthy old man who took her in and looked after her. On his death, which was not long after they began living together, Charlotte found he had provided for her in his will, leaving her enough money to become the owner of a hat shop, not just an employee in one. Charlotte was back on track with her career – until the Duke of Devonshire happened to pass by her little boutique and fall in love with her.

There were perhaps worse things that could have happened to her. The duke established Charlotte in a comfortable house with servants to wait on her, and he would come and make love to her. She may have even kept the management of her hat shop.

One woman's happiness often seems to be linked to another's despair. Charlotte had a baby girl, also named Charlotte, not long before the unsuspecting Lady Georgiana married William, the 5th Duke of Devonshire. It was no wonder that Georgiana found his embraces rather cold, as his heart was elsewhere.

Charlotte Spencer, the thorn in the new bride's side, only lived another four years, but these may have been four too many for Georgiana who, although she never mentioned any names, must have been aware of the mistress's existence. Georgiana herself was having trouble conceiving or carrying a child to full term. It would be nine years before she successfully gave birth. Therefore it must have been painful to know that her husband was enjoying fatherhood at another woman's house.

When Charlotte Spencer died, Georgiana had no objections whatsoever to the arrival at her house of her husband's illegitimate daughter. Little Charlotte became Georgiana's sweetheart, the child

Georgiana Cavendish

she could not have herself. They decided to give the child her father's Christian name, William, as a surname, altering it only slightly by adding an 's' to the end. This was common practice at the time, giving a father's name as a surname, keeping the blood ties linked while not acknowledging the relationship any more than could be avoided. In the case of Charlotte Williams, her story was that she was the orphan child of a distant relation of Georgiana's.

By the time Charlotte Williams had made her debut into the household of her father and so-called distant cousin, Georgiana had found another absorbing but expensive hobby. She had become a ruthless and compulsive gambler. She was the darling of society with her beauty and fashion, her wit and general affability. Her open friendliness and compassion for those less fortunate than herself earned Georgiana many friends in the lower classes as well as with her peers.

Probably in a bid to stem some of her hurt and loneliness, Georgiana had taken to the gaming tables, as much for social contact and to be admired and loved as for any other reason, but she was soon hooked on trying to win money. Unfortunately she lost more than she won, often exceeding her already generous allowance of £4,000 a year. The first time she found herself in real debt she applied to her parents for help. Her mother, always ready to stand by her eldest daughter, agreed to pay off the sum but only on the condition that Georgiana tell her husband about it. The duke's reaction to his wife's profligacy was extremely surprising. He paid her parents back in full and walked away, never mentioning the subject again; there was no admonishment, no outrage. Georgiana must have felt as though she was invisible to such a cool husband.

One of the greatest influences on the young duchess's life was meeting the politician Charles James Fox. He was 28 when they met in 1777 and not at all good-looking. His short, stout figure was not particularly suitable for the extravagant fashions he chose to wear, but he, like Georgiana, enjoyed attracting attention with his bizarre styles; changing his hair colour from one day to the next was one of his favourite pastimes. Charles was also a gambler and had run up debts that made Georgiana's look petty.

Apart from being lively and entertaining Charles Fox gave Georgiana intellectual stimulation and a strong, supportive friendship. It was

Elizabeth Hervey Foster

Charles who first got the duchess interested in politics. She became a devout campaigner for his party.

With motivation coming from several of her friends, including Fox, Georgiana wrote a novel, *The Sylph*, which was published anonymously in 1779 although it was attributed to 'a young lady'. The contents were often autobiographical and dealt with a loveless marriage like her own.

During a visit to Bath, for health reasons, Georgiana made friends with a young woman of social standing, Lady Elizabeth Foster, *née* Hervey. Elizabeth was the daughter of a clergyman, not a poor one as Charlotte's father had been but one who lived well beyond his means. As a younger son he had entered the Church, as was common for those being the third in line for inheritance, thinking it unlikely that he ever would inherit. At some point he was appointed the Bishop of Derry, although this did little to relieve the constant financial difficulties the family found itself in. It was as the daughter of the Bishop of Derry that Elizabeth in 1776 was married off to Irishman John Thomas Foster, a respectable man who did not feel the need for a dowry (the bishop, as a spendthrift, had nothing to offer the man who took his daughter off his hands). Mr Foster seemed to be a rather serious young man who was the opposite of his father-in-law, in money matters at least.

At the time of Elizabeth's marriage it was deemed a very good match for a penniless young woman, even if she did come from aristocratic stock. Three years after her marriage, the unexpected happened and her father inherited the title of 4th Earl of Bristol on the death of his second eldest brother who, like the eldest brother before him, had been without legitimate children. Plain Elizabeth Foster became Lady Elizabeth.

Although Elizabeth complained bitterly to her new best friend Georgiana that she had never wanted to marry John Foster, and had begged her parents not to make her accept, a different point of view had been put forward by her parents. They claimed that it was entirely a love match between the two young people and that they were only too happy to approve their daughter's choice.

If the marriage of Elizabeth Christiana Hervey to John Foster was originally a love match, by 1780 it most definitely was not. Elizabeth was pregnant with the couple's second child. Foster was accused of seducing his wife's maid and this was the story that Elizabeth's family supported when their daughter's marriage failed. Foster refused to try to reconcile and insisted on a permanent separation. Under the rules of the separation Foster enforced his right to have custody of the two children. Elizabeth was not allowed to see her two boys for fourteen years. Foster also refused to maintain his wife after their break-up. Elizabeth Foster was returned to her parents to be supported by them.

The Earl of Bristol gave his daughter an allowance of £300 a year. It was an amount that was considered well below that needed to maintain the standard of an earl's daughter. Even in this the earl was so careless with money that the allowance was not paid regularly and Elizabeth was often short of money, even for necessities.

It was as the penniless and abandoned wife of a man who had used her cruelly that Elizabeth came to be friends with Georgiana, Duchess of Devonshire. Perhaps the two young women felt an affinity through the lack of love from their spouses. The result was that during the Devonshires' time in Bath, Georgiana took it on herself to take Elizabeth Foster under her protective wing.

Elizabeth, whom Georgiana called Bess, made herself a friend of the duke's as well, and for a while she seemed to bring the couple together as they had never been before. Having Bess living in the household was both a blessing and a torment for Georgiana. When they were alone they were the best of friends, joking, laughing, sharing secrets and using nicknames for each other: Georgiana was Mrs Rat and Bess was Racky (supposedly because of her cough); they both referred to the Duke as Canis (for his love of dogs). When Georgiana's husband was at home the situation became a trifle strained. Before too long, though, as was bound to happen, Georgiana began to suspect that the duke was overly fond of Mrs Foster. Bess had been unwell with a nasty and persistent cough. The duke took an unusual interest in the welfare of his wife's companion, which Bess enjoyed very much it seems.

When Georgiana became pregnant again she was urged by her mother to take things easy, meaning in particular to stop partying so hard and to stay at home and rest. It was at this time that Bess was formally engaged by the duke and duchess to be the governess of little Charlotte, who was still very much Georgiana's darling. The governess and her charge were to go and spend the winter in the south of France. It was to be a healthy trip away for both of them, hopefully providing a cure for Bess's persistent cough.

Georgiana was very upset at the idea of both her dearest people going away from her for so long a time, but her mother, Lady Spencer, who suffered from jealousy at the friendship between her daughter and Bess, was relieved and thought she would be able to have her daughter's entire affection directed towards herself again.

Georgiana spent most of the ensuing months at home, as she'd been advised, while she awaited the birth of her baby. The duke was absolutely sure the child would be female and therefore put out that it was of no interest to him. In July 1783 Georgiana did give birth to a little girl. She, at least, was delighted with her baby and, most unusually for the time, breastfed the infant herself. It was not considered the thing to do for aristocrats, who nearly always employed a wet nurse for the purpose. Georgiana, however, probably in the absolute delight that she had successfully borne a child, was going to indulge every maternal bone in her body. The move was popular with the duchess's many fans.

In the meantime, Bess Foster was feeling left out of all the excitement and afraid that her companionship to the duchess was no longer needed now that she had a child of her own. Even the duke seemed in danger of neglecting the one-time favourite. Bess wrote letters to both duchess and duke but to the former she let it be known that she was not able to live on her meagre income. The duchess was wracked with guilt and made sure that money was sent immediately.

Bess, relieved of her financial troubles (she too had been in debt, maybe not as a gambler but because she liked to live beyond her means) was able to live comfortably in Italy and ended up taking a house in Naples, where she was reported to have been entertaining not one but two lovers. Charlotte, the duke's illegitimate daughter, was still under Bess's care.

Georgiana wrote a letter to Bess trying to assure her that she didn't believe a word of what was being said about her. Bess realised that her affairs were not as private as she had thought and had to work hard at making sure her reputation was not tarnished to such an extent that the duke and duchess dismissed her from their acquaintance (and employment). She wrote affectionate letters back to both of them and made sure she kept a lower profile while on the Continent.

In the following year Georgiana's father died and she was feeling guilty that she had not been with him when he was ill. She poured her heart out, as usual, to Bess. And then when she and her husband went to Bath, again for health reasons, they both wrote to Bess telling her how much they missed her and how different their visit was this time round without her happy company. It was not long before Georgiana was begging her friend to return home.

While she had been in France and Italy, Bess had made several romantic conquests, one of them being Cardinal Bernis and another Count Fersen, a Swedish diplomat who had the honour of being the lover of Marie Antoinette. Bess was obviously enjoying life abroad and although she did not want to sever ties with the Devonshires, she was not ready to return to their stable. Georgiana became quite agitated at Bess's procrastination in returning as requested, the latter claiming her health was not up to the trip and that Charlotte needed another year in which to become more refined and ladylike. Also, in one letter Bess commented that on her return the tongues would begin to wag again.

Georgiana countered this with a plan in which Bess would return home to them in England but would have her own residence where she would spend a respectable amount of time. She would no longer be Charlotte's governess and therefore would have the freedom to be a companion to both the Duke and duchess as commanded. Georgiana could not understand her friend's reluctance to take up such an offer.

Bess did not leave Italy until August 1784 when Georgiana finally pleaded the Duke's ill health as a reason for her to return to them in England. When Bess arrived back she was extremely thin, to an unhealthy extent. Georgiana's mother, who had always disliked Bess and distrusted her completely, suggested that she would do better to go abroad again, as obviously the English climate did not suit her.

Bess did become the subject of speculation, though not outright gossip. It was wondered what the nature of her relationship with the duke and duchess really was, but friends and relations of the married couple couldn't find anything untoward happening. Georgiana did not seem to find the solace in her friend that she thought she would, and her own suspicions about Bess and the duke began to rise again. This time they were not without foundation.

After Bess returned, her thinness began to worry Georgiana and the duke so much that they took her to London to see the eminent physicians of the day. Nothing in particular was diagnosed but the general medical opinion was that Bess needed to live in a warmer climate. She was to go back to France, Paris to be exact. She was to go without Charlotte and she would have all expenses paid and a handsome allowance.

It was while she was in Paris that Bess realised she was expecting the duke's child. It was not a welcome surprise, nor was the news that Georgiana was also pregnant again. Bess was worried about losing her friend and her reputation, and jealous at having to share the duke's attentions with Georgiana. Bess attached herself to the Duke of Dorset, becoming his mistress in Paris. Even though she had a new protector she realised she couldn't pin the pregnancy on him and that she would have to take herself somewhere quiet and out of society. She went to stay with her brother in Italy.

In September 1784 Georgiana gave birth to another daughter, Harriet. Bess was to also have a girl, Caroline Rosalie, born at an inn in rural Italy under false pretences; Bess was supposedly the wife of Louis (in reality a servant to Bess's brother John) and it was in this squalid and unfriendly place that she went into labour. She had received secret letters from the duke hinting at his concern for her but never overtly naming the cause of it. He did tell her how much he missed her and what his plans involving her were. Whether this was any consolation in her hour of need is not known.

The kindly servant, Louis, took Caroline to his own family to be brought up amongst them. This meant that Bess could visit the child and know she was being well looked after. With her mind at ease over baby Caroline, Bess returned to the social life she had been enjoying until her pregnancy began to show. One of the first things she did was to fall for the Russian Ambassador in Italy.

The duke and duchess were again letting Bess know how much they both missed her and wanted her home again with them. The duke knew what prevented Bess from accepting the offer straight away and he tried to tell her that Georgiana didn't know about them, and wouldn't get to know if he could help it, but if she did find out he told Bess that he would take all the blame. There was still Caroline to consider, however, and whatever else Bess may have been she seemed genuinely to love her children. She had already lost two to her husband. Could she bear to be parted from her third?

It wasn't until July 1786 that Bess was able to go back to England to be with her two best friends. She had managed to persuade the Comte St Jules to claim little Caroline as his daughter but to an unnamed mother. Caroline officially took his name and was made at home there. The duke went to meet Bess at Southampton on her arrival from France. Georgiana did not accompany him although other family members were there, so displays of affection were probably kept very quiet. All Bess's worries and jealousies about the duke were put aside at the reunion. What is more, the duke was suffering from his recurring gout problem and this may well have put the dampeners on any romantic activities.

Georgiana, although she did continue to have doubts about her friend's motives towards her husband, relied on Bess for support. Georgiana was frequently in financial trouble. She was still a compulsive gambler and through secretly borrowing and losing she had clocked up an enormous debt. Creditors were on her back, threatening to reveal to the duke the extent of her profligacy. One in particular was causing the duchess great agitation, a man called Martindale. Georgiana had made a deal with him over the betting table that when one of them won something over the other they could double or even treble the sum. This meant that the downward spiral for the duchess took an even faster pace.

By the time of Bess's return to the family home, Georgiana was in debt to the tune of £100,000 (around £6 million today). It is no wonder she was suffering from nervous seizures and upsets. Bess was studiously avoiding her friend, afraid of her guilt coming to the fore and bringing her comfortable situation to an end.

In September Bess's former flame, the Duke of Dorset, visited the Devonshires and began a flirtatious relationship with the duchess. Bess was not at all jealous; it meant that she commanded the Duke of Devonshire's attention. Georgiana experienced a strange illness after her admirer had left the house. It meant she stayed in her own rooms for long periods of time alone, except for her mother. While the duchess was indisposed in this way Bess took it upon herself to take over the role of mistress of the house (as well as mistress of the master).

Finally, and perhaps in order to put an end to her emotional suffering, Georgiana told her husband about the debts she owed to Martindale. She did not tell him about the other debts she had accrued. Although she expected her husband to be furious with her, she did not expect his violent declaration that he wished to be separated from her. The duchess, and her family, were devastated.

Bess, Georgiana's bosom companion, did not rush to her side to support her in her dire distress. Perhaps she wondered whether Georgiana's removal from her husband's side might benefit her own agenda. Would she be able to step into Georgiana's shoes, to run the household and have the duke to herself? The big hitch in this plan was that the duke still wanted a legitimate heir and in order to do that he needed to maintain his marriage to Georgiana and, of course, access to her bed.

Bess realised that to be the duke's mistress, publicly acknowledged, was probably not the course she wanted things to take. It would mean she would become a social pariah and, although she might have the duke, she would not have the parties and social status that she loved and craved. Bess decided she would wait.

In the end, nothing happened. Georgiana stayed as head of her own house and continued to sleep with the duke, as her position demanded. The duke, in what seems to be absolutely characteristic of his natural apathy, let the matter drop, almost as if he had forgotten about it or had tired of it. He appeared to enjoy domestic comfort and for that to happen he had to have both his wife and his mistress – and the two women were expected to get along and be happy. For her part Georgiana genuinely loved Bess and relied on her for companionship and to help her communicate with her husband. Bess, although not happy in sharing her lover, did appreciate the friendship of the duchess and the society into which such a friendship led her.

A plan was made to help Georgiana get out of debt (although only for the amount she had confessed to); limits were put on her allowance and the time she could spend in London, in order to limit further damage being made at the gaming tables.

In 1788 Bess conceived another child. She declared it was the Duke of Devonshire's but there has always been some doubt, because at the time the Duke of Richmond was making unmistakable advances in her direction. It is thought that Bess may have been stringing him along as well. Bess told Georgiana about the pregnancy, not hiding it and suffering as she had done before. The time had long passed since the two women pretended they didn't know what was happening between each of them and the duke. Georgiana wanted to go with Bess to France to be with her during the confinement. However, Lady Spencer intervened, hinting to her daughter that she was worried that if she was alone in France she may well be tempted to fall in with the Duke of Dorset (with whom she had already had a dalliance) who resided there. Thus Georgiana stayed at home and played the dutiful wife. Bess had her baby, a boy whom she named appropriately so that his paternity was suggested without being overtly stated, Augustus William James Clifford. The second and last names, both being Cavendish names, hinted at the boy's father.

During Bess's trip away something happened to Georgiana: a young man called Charles Grey fell madly in love with her and she with him. Whether anything came of it at this point, other than a flattering flirtation, is uncertain. However, something certainly happened later on ...

A year after the birth of little Augustus William, the happy trio of Georgiana, the duke and Bess set out for France. The duke wanted to take health treatment at Spa, Georgiana was hoping it would help her to conceive a baby boy and Bess wanted to see her two youngest children. It was not a good time to travel in France; the revolution was on its way and violence was already breaking out. They did not stay in Paris for long but made their way to Spa. Before leaving the city Georgiana paid a private farewell to her dear, faithful friend Marie Antoinette, who had supported the duchess throughout a decade and a half of marital trauma, rejection, miscarriages and the permanent inclusion of Bess into the intimate household. Georgiana and the Queen of France would not meet again.

Another concern was the welfare of the duke's two illegitimate daughters and his illegitimate infant son who had been left in Paris: Charlotte by his first mistress, and Caroline and Augustus William by Bess. With the help of their long-term family friend James Hare, Charlotte and Caroline were carried to Spa to be with their parents (so to speak). The duke's longed-for son, who unfortunately had to remain a secret, did not make it to England until 1791, when he was placed with a family living in Somerset.

In September 1789, while the Devonshires were still in Spa, Georgiana discovered she was indeed pregnant. She was anxious to return home and away from the violence but her husband forbade her to travel, fearful it might induce miscarriage.

In December the duke returned to England, leaving his two women to care for each other in France. Neither of them was happy about his leaving them there. Lady Spencer had travelled over to Brussels, where the little party had ended up staying until a house was made available for Georgiana and her retinue just outside of Paris. The city itself was subdued. In May 1790 Georgiana went into labour and Bess was swiftly packed off to the opera by an anxious Lady Spencer – so that witnesses would see her in public as there had been rampant speculation about which of 'the two Mrs Devonshires' was really pregnant. The English aristocracy did not want to have a swift swap pulled on them and be forced to accept as the true heir of Devonshire a boy who was really the son of the duke's mistress.

Georgiana finally gave birth to the son and heir of the Duke of Devonshire. Her health was poor after all their trials and it wasn't until well into June that her life was considered to be out of danger and the longed for trip home was able to be planned. They travelled back to England in August.

While everything seemed set to relax into its previous harmonious threesome, Lady Spencer was bent on having Bess put firmly in her place. Georgiana's mother had befriended Selina Trimmer, the children's governess, while they were all in France and she used the young woman to spy on Bess and to help turn the household staff against her. When Georgiana finally noticed what was happening she was furious and wrote a stern letter to her mother stating that Bess was part of her and her husband's life and that was a fact. She said that by trying to upset the balance Lady Spencer was in fact only hurting her daughter. Georgiana was not well. She was also still in serious debt and worrying over it. Lady Spencer, worried for her daughter, desisted in tormenting Bess.

Georgiana was soon to entertain another greater worry. She had begun a real affair with Charles Grey, who claimed he ardently loved her. It was when she was in Bath with Bess and the children, helping nurse her ill younger sister Harriet, that Georgiana discovered she was pregnant and that the child had to be Grey's. Hoping to keep the indiscretion a secret by having the birth abroad, and without her husband ever knowing she'd been carrying it, Georgiana and Bess were planning to accompany a still ailing Harriet to balmy Cornwall. But the trio were found out before they left Bath. The duke surprised them with a visit after he had been tipped off that all was not right with his family.

The duke was furious. He ranted and raved at his wife but was also very angry with Bess for having helped cover up the crime. He threatened to divorce Georgiana; then he made ultimatums. Eventually he settled on Georgiana having the baby abroad and that Bess, Harriet and Lady Spencer would go with her. The child was to be given up for adoption immediately, otherwise he would divorce Georgiana without further ado and take complete custody of their three children; if she didn't give up Grey's baby then she would never see her children again. The whole household was terribly upset by this but Georgiana couldn't see any other way out of it. What is more, the company was denied any extra money from the duke to help ease their troubles.

In February 1791 Georgiana gave birth to yet another girl and called her Eliza. She had no chance to nurse the baby; it was whisked off to a foster home before being put in the care of Charles Grey's family in Northumberland. Little Eliza was not loved by her grandparents and was only allowed to see Georgiana on special visits to London. The child thought that Georgiana was her godmother, but it was not long before Georgiana's secret slipped out in the form of malicious gossip. In a cruel twist, the duchess was prevented from nurturing Eliza because it would cause embarrassment to her husband – but everyone knew about it anyway.

Although Georgiana was not permitted to let Eliza know she was the girl's true mother, her legitimate children knew from before Eliza's birth who she was. They were allowed to see their little half-sister but were sternly reminded never to let slip that they were related. Eliza was brought up to believe that Charles was her brother, not her father. The girl's grandparents were not unkind to her, but Georgiana and others who saw her at home felt that Eliza was largely ignored by the family and unloved by them.

The friendship between Georgiana and her husband's mistress seemed only to grow. Whether there was still jealousy between them is unlikely at this stage. Georgiana had been cruelly treated by the man she was legally bound to live with, but whom had never loved her. Bess was probably chastened by her friend's punishment and probably thanked her lucky stars that she had never been caught in one of her little romantic adventures away from the duke.

The two women stuck together. It was because Bess had stood by her so faithfully that Georgiana went with her friend so she could get the Comte St Jules to sign the adoption papers for Caroline and make her his heir.

Georgiana was not free to return home until her husband said she could. He did not write to his wife nor did he write to Bess very much either; both women were under a dark and heavy cloud. They were told to wait on the Continent until he came in person to accompany them home; it would be at his leisure that such a thing would occur. France was in turmoil and in 1793 Louis XVI was executed, followed not long afterwards by his wife. The incident meant that Britain, in disgust, sent the French Ambassador home and, in retaliation, France declared war on England. Georgiana and her retinue were in relative safety in Naples, although very keen to get home.

Still the duke did not give his women leave to come home, even though he was probably feeling rather lonely. Finally, in May 1793, Georgiana received word that she could go home, although the duke did not travel to the Continent to accompany them. Her sister Harriet, however, was ill again when they got to Rome and was forced to stay, convalescing there with their mother. Georgiana and Bess soldiered on through all the upheaval in Europe until they got to Ostend. All the boats were full and it seemed as though the two women would be left behind. Luckily, an old acquaintance of the duchess offered them a place on his private boat and so they were able to leave the turmoil behind and head for home.

The duke, surprisingly, met them at Dartford and gave them a very warm welcome. He even went as far as presenting Georgiana with a brand new coach to have her carried home in. They had been away from home for two years and it was quite odd that he had left them for so long overseas.

There were good things and bad things awaiting Georgiana at Devonshire House. Her children had been affected by her two-year absence, the eldest becoming withdrawn and clingy for her mother and the little boy unable to recognise her. The duke had made himself more or less into an invalid who needed constant care; his wife, determined not to be banished again, tried hard to make a new life for herself with him. Bess was now the one out of favour. The duke felt she had betrayed him in helping his wife. He did not dismiss her from the family, and he still kept her in his bed, but it was more because Georgiana willed it that Bess was able to continue as she had for so many years.

Upon her return, Georgiana found Charles Grey wanting to renew their relationship. She was tempted, it's true, but after her heartbreaking ordeal over Eliza she strictly forbade herself to give into the temptation and told her suitor directly what she felt. Not long afterwards, in the following year, Charles Grey became engaged to Mary Ponsonby; Georgiana, to whom he had declared an undying passion, discovered the news from sources other than himself. Georgiana presented a brave and disinterested public face, assuring those close to her that she felt nothing but joy for the couple.

In 1796 Georgiana, who had been suffering from bad headaches, finally found she was too ill to go about her everyday business. Her eye had swollen horribly and she couldn't stand light. She was ill for weeks and underwent all sorts of drastic treatments. At her bedside were the ever faithful Bess and Harriet. When she was able to get about again Georgiana took life very quietly and slowly. Her face was ravaged, one eye left drooping, and she was bone thin. It would have been difficult to have seen in her the former beauty and elegance.

Bess, on the other hand, was finding she was getting a lot more attention and interest. She no longer had her dear friend to overshadow her in looks nor at social events. And, what's more, Bess's estranged husband had suddenly died leaving her a small fortune and the freedom to be reunited with her two oldest children. Georgiana bade Bess to have the boys, now in their teens, to come and visit her at Devonshire House.

Bess became preoccupied with the idea that her lover, the Duke of Richmond, also recently widowed, would pop the question of marriage to her at any time. Georgiana, however, was not keen to lose her best friend, confidante and her husband's solace, knowing that life would become so difficult if Bess got a life of her own.

The Duke of Richmond and Bess decided it would not be prudent to get engaged so soon after their spouses' deaths and declared they would not do so until a twelve-month period of decent mourning had passed. Bess, although acknowledging the debt she owed to the Devonshires, was still anxious to be someone in her own right and to have the kind of life that Georgiana had had: money, social standing and a title.

But poor Bess was not going to be made an offer in a hurry. She was constantly expecting a proposition of marriage by Richmond but it never came. By 1802 she had had enough of waiting and enough of being the sounding board for all Georgiana's woes, she wanted a life of her own and she went to France in search of it, taking her daughter Caroline and one of her legitimate sons. As soon as she had left Georgiana began writing her usual letters telling Bess how much she missed her.

In France, Bess was not just there for pleasure. She was also nursing her niece who was dying of tuberculosis. Then she had to return to England because France was threatening war. Unable to make it as an independent woman, she retreated to the only home she had really known, just in time to nurse Georgiana who was suffering from kidney stones, and the duke who was suffering from all sorts of imagined illnesses. More trips to Bath and seaside health resorts ensued, with Bess playing the ever concerned nursemaid whilst hiding her own extreme disappointment in not becoming the Duchess of Richmond.

The cyclical nature of the relationship between Bess and the duchess and duke was to bring Georgiana's debts to the fore again.

Added to her poor health, and the duke's, the duchess's gambling debts had never truly been resolved. Again it was Bess who was asked to broach the subject with the duke. By this time, 1804, the duke was probably not so intimately active with his mistress. He did seem to be an extraordinary creature of habit and didn't like his little threesome being disturbed or broken up in anyway. Perhaps the duke had mellowed with middle age and ill health, or perhaps he wanted to continue a smooth and peaceful life; whichever it was, when Bess told him that Georgiana had debts of up to £50,000 or more, he hardly turned a hair. Without rebuke Georgiana's husband put in place a financial system that would pay off creditors, keep her in style and comfort, and would not cripple the estate. It is not said anywhere that he showed anything but kindness and sympathy for his wife.

In March 1806 Georgiana succumbed to yet another illness. It was not a fit of nerves, not kidney stones and it was not imagined. To the doctors of the day it was a complete mystery, although now it is thought she had an abscess on her liver. On 30 March 1806 Georgiana, Duchess of Devonshire, died in the presence of her best friend Bess, her sister Harriet and her husband, all united in mourning her death.

This was the end of Georgiana's part in the strange story of the Devonshires. Without Georgiana around to take her part in matters Bess felt vulnerable to attack by other family members. The duke was still her faithful friend, possibly her lover, but he was always in need of being looked after. In Georgiana's will she had made Bess the keeper of all her private papers. It was a move calculated to keep Bess within the family circle as it would take a long time for her to go through them and organise them. And, who knew what secrets Bess would then have in her knowledge?

Just as everyone (except the duke) feared, Bess not only took on her role as archivist of the duchess's extensive correspondence and literary works, she automatically stepped into her shoes as female head of the household. This suited the duke, who did not want the hassle of having to find a substitute, but Lady Spencer and Georgiana's daughters were all put out by it.

Finally, in 1809, a decent interval after Georgiana's death, the Duke of Devonshire announced that he was engaged to be married to Lady Elizabeth Foster, Bess. The family were outraged, although they had known it might happen.

Bess had her wish at last, to become the wife of someone important, to have a title that meant something and with it automatic respect (or at least the show of it).

What she perhaps didn't bargain for was that the duke, being true to his nature, had taken a fancy to a much younger woman, another Spencer, and had begun to involve her in family affairs. It looked as though he was trying to reconstruct the ménage a trois that had kept him comfortable for nearly thirty years. However, Bess doesn't seem to have been too troubled by the duke's interest in the young Mrs Spencer: she had what she wanted.

Nevertheless, she did not have her duke as husband for very long. He died within three years of their marriage, in 1811. With the duke's death the title moved to his heir, William George Cavendish Hartington, known as Hart to the family. Bess had to retire and, after a public fuss over what she was and wasn't entitled to, moved to Rome, where she had other lovers. In 1824, exactly eighteen years after Georgiana's death, Bess also died. Her body was returned to England and put in the grave alongside her two best friends, Georgiana and William Devonshire, along with Harriet, the duchess's younger faithful sister.

Part 4
The Notion of Free Love

Because women, and married women in particular, had such a hard time of it in the eighteenth and nineteenth centuries – not being able to own property, being the property of their husbands, not having the right to custody of their children and so on – there were some men and women who felt this imbalance needed to be righted. Marriage was being seen by some women as a legal form of slavery – and the idea of any woman wanting to enslave herself in that way was preposterous. These were radical thinkers of the time – and most conventional, respectable people were horrified by some of their notions.

If marriage held so many negatives aspects for women, why should they bother marrying? Why not live with the man they love and keep their freedom as well? The people who put forward such ideas were not talking about mistresses or a substitute marriage but a companionship in which both partners were equal. It also meant that when affection left a relationship the couple would be free to break apart and set up with another lover.

Mary Wollstonecraft, the mother of Mary Shelley, was one such thinker. As a wife one gave up all reason to exist at all, she claimed. She thought women needed to have more equality in their relationships and she tried to practise what she believed in. It was not as easy as it looked in theory. She found herself in one relationship in which she wanted stability and monogamy but the man did not. She had an illegitimate child with him. She later married the philosopher

Mary Wollstonecraft

William Godwin who shared her views on marriage, yet they got married in order to legitimise the birth of their daughter Mary.

Wollstonecraft's and Godwin's ideas influenced at least one, if not several, generations. It was certainly time for a change to the laws concerning marriage, women's rights, property ownership and custody of children. It does not seem, however, that those enlightened individuals who proscribed to the practice of free love actually thought of the consequences, such as children and broken hearts, when they used it as a licence to sleep with whoever took their fancy. Free love needed to be guided by common sense and fair play.

TWO FRIENDS, TWO MISTRESSES

Harriet Taylor (and John Stuart Mill) and Lizzie Flower (and William Johnson Fox) were best friends. Harriet was a married woman with a family and Lizzie was the young ward of an older married man.

Harriet Taylor was born in 1807 and by the age of 18 or 19 had married a man eleven years her senior, the respectable but dull John Taylor. Four years after her marriage, and as a mother of two boys, Harriet and her husband gave a dinner party. It was a large gathering and was made up of some of London's most promising thinkers. One of the guests, the Unitarian Minister William Johnson Fox, brought a world-weary young man with him: John Stuart Mill. Mill had been brought up to be an intellectual and a scholar, having experienced a lonely and loveless childhood, being expected to achieve greatness through study and the use of intellect but to ignore the needs of his heart. He was said to have been reading Greek by the time he was 4.

Harriet Taylor was a member of Fox's congregation at the South Place Chapel, and it was to him she made a confession of loneliness despite being married. It may or may not have been Fox's intention for the two young people to meet. It is hardly likely that he wanted to start an affair between them (and it isn't certain that Harriet and Mill had any kind of sexual relationship with each other before John Taylor's death in 1849).

Harriet was no shrinking violet and had already been writing about women's rights and position in society. Fox had encouraged her in her intellectual pursuits and so had Harriet Martineau, an established thinker and writer of her time. Martineau was an interesting woman who many considered extremely ugly. She was also very deaf, having to use an ear trumpet to aid her. When she was young she had lost her sense of taste and smell and had gradually lost most of her hearing too. She was also a member of the Unitarian church community, which was how she came to be a friend of Harriet Taylor's.

Mill, in his early twenties, was ready to fall in love. Harriet Taylor, considered as beautiful as Harriet Martineau was considered ugly, must have shone like a gem next to her friend. It would not have been difficult for the young Mill to fall for her. Harriet for her part was feeling starved of excitement. Her poor husband was really a very good man: he was wealthy (always a happy characteristic), he had the same religious (Unitarian) beliefs that his wife had, he also supported the political reforms that she approved of. Yet Harriet confided to Fox that her husband was still not enough for her intellectual appetite.

In some of Harriet's writings on women and marriage it is plain that she does not think that women get a fair deal. In one letter she writes that women are brought up with only one end in mind, to get married. She states that there are many women who find themselves without the benefit of having had a ceremony in church. Harriet's conclusion is that they do not seem to suffer any more or less than those who are wed in the eyes of God. The letter continues to say that by setting marriage as a woman's main goal in life, by actually going through the process and becoming a wife she in fact loses her very existence. Harriet was married to a man who was worthy, fair and probably truly loved his beautiful wife, but it doesn't seem true that she reciprocated the feelings. For Harriet Taylor, being a wife and mother was not enough. This is not by any means a judgement on her. Even though we may feel sorry for John Taylor, whose main fault seems dullness, we can sympathise with a young woman who realises that she has achieved everything that was ever expected of her and she is not yet 25. If Harriet had known how it would be, she may well have followed the example of the other Harriet, the writer Martineau. Harriet Martineau achieved a miraculous amount of money for a woman writer in the nineteenth century, certainly enough to keep her living comfortably. However, the other Harriet had already made a choice and it seemed there was no way out of it.

When John Mill stepped onto the scene, Harriet Taylor began to bloom. Friends and relations of the pair must have known that the growing attachment was more than mere friendship. And when Harriet finally told her husband that she was in love with another man, although he was devastated it could hardly have been a surprise. John Taylor asked his wife to give up her lover.

In the meantime, Harriet's best friend, another lively young woman, Eliza Flower, was having relationship issues of her own. She and her sister Sarah were made the wards of William Johnson Fox, Harriet Taylor's friend and the minister of her church. The sisters' father, Benjamin Flower, had been an outspoken journalist and a friend of Fox's. On Flower's death, Fox became the guardian for both girls. Sarah, the elder sister, became a poet, married and more or less left the scene. Eliza was a musician and went on to become a reputable composer. After her sister left the Fox's home, Eliza (known as Lizzie) became her guardian's mistress. Fox still had a wife with whom he had children.

Fox and Lizzie attempted to keep their affair secret, at least within the confines of the family home. Mrs Fox was, understandably, very unhappy about the situation and moved into another part of the house. She also demanded Fox get a legal separation. Fox declined, stating that the process was too expensive. In desperation the poor woman went to her friends, who were also members of her husband's congregation, and poured her heart out to them. The result was an enormous scandal. The church community divided between their minister, Fox, and his injured spouse. Harriet Taylor and John Mill took Fox's side in the debate. It was thought that a clergyman accused of adultery (and with his ward) would have had a hard time to keep his post, but to the amazement of many of his friends Fox managed to keep his position. Fox and Lizzie found a new home, leaving his wife and children in the old one and, even though Fox said he couldn't afford it, he had to pay them a settlement fee.

While Harriet and Mill had remained faithful supporters of Fox and Lizzie, they did not follow their friends' example. Fox urged them to follow suit. If it was all right for him then why should they not do the same?

Mill may have been keen to set up house with Harriet but she didn't feel she could just dump her loyal and loving husband. Perhaps for Harriet marriage was, after all, something more than a contract in which a woman lost all sense of self. She did care for her husband and she knew he was already hurting because she loved someone else. He was also a kind man and the couple had three children.

Harriet's husband came up with a solution that may not have been the perfect answer but one that certainly gave them all a bit of relief. He had a house set up for Harriet in Kent, where she could live with her baby daughter; John Taylor and the two boys would visit her regularly. At other times, usually at the weekends, John Mill would visit her as well. Whether the two men were able to keep out of each other's way is not known, but it must have worked to a reasonable extent.

Mill was not content. He wanted Harriet to himself and he wanted to show her off to his friends in society. Yet society would not tolerate it and their one excursion into the London social scene was not a success. While nothing was said during the party, the host pulled Mill aside afterwards and told him it was not done and would not be tolerated. Mill's friendship with the host dissolved shortly afterwards. The couple did not try to go out again. Not only was it a social problem to been seen out and about with someone else's wife, it was not in the best interests of an aspiring politician.

In 1838 Mill and Harriet were allowed a holiday together in Naples. Harriet's husband had escorted her to Paris, supposedly to make it look like a respectable family vacation. After a short time in Paris with Harriet and young Helen (their daughter), John Taylor went home to his boys and business. The other John took up where the husband left off and he and Harriet, and Helen, spent three months together.

Mill always maintained that he and Harriet did not have a sexual relationship while she was still married to John Taylor. This may or may not have been the case. It does seem rather unlikely that the two of them, so in love and on their own, would not give in to a passion that had led to such odd living circumstances of the Taylor household. This way of living for the three of them went on for nearly twenty years and ended only with John Taylor's death in 1849.

Harriet Taylor took two years to mourn her dead husband: leaving a respectable period before she married her lover was at least one last thing she could do for him. In 1851 Harriet threw aside her widow's weeds and married John Mill. There were rumours flying around town that he had only stuck with Harriet for so long so that he could get his hands on the other man's extensive wealth, but it seems he was really after Harriet, which, no doubt, John Taylor would have considered his most prized jewel.

The marriage made the pair respectable at last. They could, if they wanted to, appear at parties together, but they chose not to. They lived a very quiet life together, talking and writing, the kind of life Harriet had dreamed of. Her children certainly did not resent the marriage and became the couple's only family, as all their other relatives had washed their hands of them.

In 1858 Harriet died. Mill lived on for at least a decade after her death, still writing and dedicating works to her. He did not marry again. Helen Taylor, Harriett's daughter by her first husband, had always been a supporter of her mother and Mill and helped him with his work on women's rights for fifteen years after her mother's death, in fact until Mill's death in 1873.

And what happened to Lizzie Flower and William Johnson Fox? They continued to live together until their deaths, which both occurred in 1846. It has been long said that the relationship was chaste, but this seems unlikely.

THE ROMANTIC POETS AND A TALE OF TWO SISTERS

Mary Wollstonecraft Shelley and Claire Clairmont were brought together when Mary's widowed father married Claire's mother who lived next door. The two girls were about the same age and both very young when their respective parents got together. What bound them together over the years was their mutual affection for the poet Percy Bysshe Shelley. The friendship between the women waxed and waned. Claire was jealous of Mary's and Shelley's relationship, Mary was jealous of Claire spending time alone with Shelley. Claire wanted more attention: she wasn't as pretty as Mary, she wasn't as clever, and she was not the daughter of two revolutionary thinkers. The lives of these two sisters are inextricably entwined and to talk about one means including the other. As they were both mistresses of married men they are each suitably qualified to have their stories told here, but for the sake of clarity it will be told as one tale.

Mary Wollstonecraft Shelley is probably most well known as the author of *Frankenstein*, she is probably next well known as the second wife of the Romantic poet Percy Bysshe Shelley. She is also, as the first of her two names suggest, the daughter of the women's rights advocate, Mary Wollstonecraft. As the daughter of Wollstonecraft and William Godwin, the radical philosopher, Mary was the heiress to some very avant-garde ideas and was brought up in an atmosphere of liberty and independence. Mary's mother died shortly after her birth, leaving her and another daughter from a previous relationship, Fanny, for Godwin to bring up on his own. Despite Godwin's ideals about love and marriage, he took a second wife, Mary Jane Vial, or Clairmont as she preferred to be called (it is unlikely that Mary Jane had ever been married to the man whose surname she used, although it may have belonged to one of her lovers). Mary Jane already had two children, a son and a daughter, both of whom were illegitimate. It is doubtful that Mary Jane was the wicked stepmother that Mary Godwin made her out to be; certainly Fanny Imlay, Mary's half-sister on her mother's side (and

Percy Bysshe Shelley

therefore unrelated by blood to either Godwin or Mary Jane) told her sister not to be cruel to their stepmother as she didn't deserve it. Mary was the favourite child of her father, while his second wife was devoted to her own children. Poor Fanny was the one who was really left out, Godwin was not her natural father and Mary Jane was not her mother; Fanny was the quietest and most conventional of the lot and the one who was left to look after both parents when Mary and Jane had disappeared with Shelley. As children, the three girls and Charles, the eldest of the two Clairmonts, got on very well together. Charles and Fanny (unrelated by blood) were so fond of Mary and Jane that when Godwin banned them from visiting the tainted Shelley household, the two of them would sneak out and do what they could to help their sisters.

As a child and teenager Mary Godwin was precocious. She already had a published work by the time she was 12. She could travel long distances by herself and was at ease in new and mixed company. Growing up in her father's house Mary was exposed to many of the philosophers, writers and leading thinkers of the day. She could converse just as happily with men older than her father or not much older than herself.

Jane Vial Clairmont – a name that she later changed to Claire Clairmont and became known by – was the illegitimate daughter of Mary Vial and an unknown man, that is until 2010 when it came to light that her natural father was John Lethbridge of Sandhill Park in Somerset (he was not, however, the father of Jane's brother). Jane was an attractive girl, dark haired and buxom with a lovely singing voice. It would be unfair to say she was uneducated or dull, she was neither, but it may well be that her stepsister outshone her. Also, poor Jane did not have that one fascinating feature that Mary had: she was not the daughter of Mary Wollstonecraft and William Godwin.

The poet Percy Bysshe Shelley had become an acquaintance of William Godwin while Mary was away in Scotland. Shelley and Godwin were busy hatching plans for accessing some of Shelley's inheritance so that it could be lent to Godwin and relieve him of deep debt. When Godwin's beautiful, clever, 16-year-old daughter burst onto the scene back in her father's house in London, Shelley suddenly increased his visits.

Shelley had long been an admirer of Godwin's work and, as an inexperienced teenager, he liked to let everyone know where he stood on the subject of marriage. To Shelley it was deemed an incarceration; it shackled couples together for a life sentence when all passion, if there ever had been any, had long since died. It is rather extraordinary then, that after having embarked on a steamy correspondence with Harriet Westbrook, a schoolmate of his sister – in response to her cries for help he had taken it upon his teenage self to rescue her – they eloped to Scotland and were married. England at the time would not allow a 16-year-old girl to marry without her parents' permission.

On their way to the border, the young couple dropped in on Shelley's friend Thomas Jefferson Hogg to ask for some money. During their month-long honeymoon in Edinburgh, Hogg discovered that against all the odds, Mr and Mrs Shelley seemed as though they might make excellent lifelong companions. Harriet was keen to impress her husband and knuckled down to a serious regime of study. They read, wrote, translated and talked. Shelley was keen for all his women to learn foreign languages: Greek, Latin, French, Italian and German. Harriet was no exception.

Back in England the repercussions of a hasty marriage on no income began to assert itself. Although Shelley would inherit handsomely on his father's death, until that time he was as dependent on his father's goodwill as any profligate son. He installed his new bride in lodgings and went off to Sussex to try to get access to some of his inheritance through the intervention of his uncle. During his absence Harriet was left in the care of Thomas Hogg who, as a friend of Shelley's, also subscribed to his philosophy on free love. With Shelley conveniently out of the way Hogg made a move on Harriet, who was appalled. On Shelley's return she told him what had happened. Shelley, preferring to take his new bride's side, wrote to Hogg chastising him for trying to seduce Harriet, telling his friend he thought his actions to be sneaky and underhand.

In order that the couple's first child, a daughter, Ianthe, should be considered legitimate, Shelley and Harriet underwent a second marriage in case their Scottish vows were not considered legal. For a man who didn't believe in marriage, marrying once seemed a bit hypocritical, but then to marry the same woman a second time, so that their daughter should be legitimate, seems extra hypocritical. Shelley's supposed disgust at marriage was for those very social reasons that he was now giving in to: social status and acceptance.

Just prior to his second marriage to Harriet, Shelley had met Mary Godwin. For Shelley it was love at first sight and may well have been for Mary as well. In contrast to the bright young, intellectual attractions of Mary Godwin was the deadening pall of marriage and fatherhood. Shelley was tiring of his young wife and her demands for attention and stability. Shelley saw this as a stifling of his creative faculties and began to resent Harriet and Ianthe. However, the Godwin's were not very happy with the state of affairs when it became obvious that Mary was falling for Shelley, and vice versa.

The Godwins were liberal thinkers. William and Mary had explored ideas about marriage and what it meant for women's rights and the freedom of the individual. However, when it became known to Godwin that his favourite offspring was falling in love with a man who was not only married but had one child and another on the way, his thoughts on free love began to waiver. It was one thing to talk about these things and another to witness the realities that accompanied them. While Shelley and Mary Godwin were relishing their new and profound love, Harriet, the abandoned pregnant spouse, was suffering extremely from hurt and fear of being left alone with two children to provide for. Without being too judgemental towards Shelley and Mary Godwin, it is hard not to think that by following one's own passions at the cost of another's the rights of that other person are diminished. In short, William Godwin forbade his daughter to continue relations with Shelley, and the young poet was banned from visiting the Godwin household.

Trying to put an embargo on Mary was futile. She, aided by her stepsister Jane Clairmont (later known as Claire Clairmont), connived to see Shelley frequently outside the house. One of their favourite trysting places was the graveyard of the Old St Pancras Church where Mary Wollstonecraft, Mary Godwin's mother, was buried. It is suggested that it was in the shade of her mother's grave that Mary lost her virginity to Shelley and conceived their first child. Jane was the lookout as well as the supposed chaperone. It has long

Mary Shelley

been speculated as to what young Jane got out of the adventure. It is possible that she was in love with Shelley herself, or that she longed for a similar grand passion. Perhaps she was just bored or lonely. Whichever it was, Jane Clairmont became an almost permanent attachment to Mary and Shelley throughout their lives.

In 1814, towards the end of July, the two sisters eloped with Shelley. He had a hackney coach wait at the end of the street at about 5 a.m. Two cloaked figures slipped out of the house in Skinner Street and boarded the vehicle with the waiting Shelley inside. He had left his wife, pregnant with their second child, and had arranged for himself, Mary and Jane to flee to Dover so they could take a boat to Calais, well out of reach of angry fathers or abandoned spouses. When Jane was an old lady she wrote that she had gone with Mary and Shelley only because she was tricked into it and had been very reluctant to continue with the journey when she discovered what they were truly about. This seems highly unlikely and the story would appear to be Jane's attempts to bring a semblance of respectability to her own youth.

Shelley's constant problem was lack of money and he certainly had none to spare when he ran away with the Godwin girls. On arriving in Dover he had to break it to them that he couldn't afford a proper passage for them to travel to Calais and the three of them ended up making the crossing in an open boat. Mary was seasick, which Shelley found touching and revelled in holding her in his arms for the entire journey. It is possible that she was already pregnant by this time and the seasickness was compounded by morning sickness.

The trio hadn't been in Calais for a day before they'd been tracked down by a furious Mrs Godwin in pursuit of her errant daughter Jane. Mary had made her own bed and could stay in it at far as Jane's mother was concerned; the two had never got along. But Jane was not going to be allowed to sink off the social pages through her sister's indiscretions. Jane at first agreed to go home with her mother, and perhaps she should have, it might well have prevented a life of heartache to come. Before they left for Dover Jane had changed her mind more than once. In the end she stayed with Mary and Shelley (which rather gives the lie to her later claim that she had been duped into the trip) while Mrs Godwin returned home a very angry and bitter woman.

Claire Clairmont

When the elopement was discovered in England Harriet was absolutely distraught. Shelley answered her pleading letters with self-righteous ones full of indignation and blame. He claimed Harriet was being clingy and selfish, denying him the happiness of being with his one true love. She should, knowing his views on marriage and free love, be pleased for him. Harriet soon gave up on getting him back and moved home to her father with her two children, a boy and a girl.

Paris was the first stop on the agenda for the threesome's tour of Europe. There Shelley managed to get the sum of £60 from English bankers. It was not a lot for three people to go on holiday with, even by the standards of those times. To save money they decided to walk throughout Europe, yet none of them was fit for the enterprise. The girls were only used to strolling in the city and Shelley, suffering from his self-imposed strict vegetarian diet, was not the strongest or most fit young man to be making the trip.

Not only were they physically disadvantaged for such a journey but Europe in 1814 was not a safe place for tourists. Only four months before, much of it had been impossible for genteel travellers and had been so since the French Revolution some twenty years earlier. What the three witnessed affected them. They saw poverty and depression, starvation and hardship as none of them had ever known. The living conditions in which they found themselves also left a lot to be desired. One night Jane refused to sleep in her own bed because the place was overrun by rats; of course this may have been a ploy to get into bed with her sister and Shelley, or to at least break up their cosiness.

They hadn't been travelling very long when Shelley took a tumble and sprained his ankle. Thus walking was out of the question and for a while they travelled by hired carriage, a luxury they could not afford. It took them as far as the Swiss border and then left them to make their own way into Switzerland. About this time Mary and Shelley embarked on a joint diary. Jane, in her typical jealous fashion, feeling deliberately left out, demanded paper from them so she could make her own journal. Mary and Shelley were finding the third in their company a burden, or at least Mary did. Shelley's relationship with Jane has never been fully fathomed. There has always been speculation that they had an on-off sexual relationship throughout Shelley's life. Years later Shelley acknowledged paternity of a little girl, Elena Adelaide. It was almost certainly not Mary's child, but there were rumours it may have been Jane's (or Claire's as she was called by then). It may be that the child was not related to any of them but was adopted and brought in to help ease Mary's sense of loss at her own daughter Clara and her son William.

In Switzerland, whatever Shelley thought, Mary was heartily sick of her sister and got Shelley to have words with her about her behaviour. Jane would not have taken this kindly and continued to go out of her way to make life miserable for Mary. Shelley, on the other hand, seemed to be enjoying the jaunt very much. He would act impulsively and erratically. One time he tried to buy a child he saw on the road and was most put out when the father told him to clear off.

Shelley certainly lived for his own pleasure, without over concern for anyone else's. By this time the £60 was all gone and they were destitute again. Shelley wrote to Harriet asking for money. He suggested she might like to bring them the money and join them in their travels. It is amazing to think that after his cavalier treatment of his pregnant wife Shelley really thought she would buy into that one. Why would a conventional young woman, dumped by her philandering husband when she was expecting their second child, want to travel through war-torn Europe in order to help out that same husband, his mistress and her sister? Did Shelley believe his attractions were that strong? Or was he naive and really believed that Harriet would fit in with the other two women?

The upshot was, of course, that Harriet refused his request. Shelley and his companions were forced to return to England. Jane didn't understand why they had to leave after they had only just got to Switzerland. She refused to believe it was for financial reasons and preferred to suggest it was her sister's fussiness over a stove in their rented dwelling that sparked off a fit of pique.

The return journey was begun one month after the elopement. On one of the barges they travelled on they managed to horrify their fellow travellers by talking revolution and how they wanted to cut off the king's head. It was a way of passing an uncomfortable time, but unfortunately smacks of juvenile delinquency and boredom.

Shelley, Mary and Jane wandered into London in early September. The captain of the boat in which they took passage was suspicious of the three and sent one of his crew to follow them home to make sure they paid for their trip. In view of their financial crisis Shelley made straight for Harriet's father's house. The two girls stayed hidden in a coach while Shelley went inside to plead with his wife for funds. Somehow he managed to persuade the injured woman to cover all his outstanding debts from money he had previously given her. Perhaps he used those very laws he didn't believe in – their marriage – as means to pressure her to do so. As Shelley's lawful wife, everything Harriet owned actually belonged, by law, to him. The boatman was paid and Shelley departed to find suitable shelter for the girls.

The Godwins refused to have them enter their house and also prohibited Charles and Fanny from visiting the trio. Shelley was furious, using Godwin's own words on freedom and love to show what a hypocrite the older man was. Godwin had sold out on his own philosophy when he married Mary Wollstonecraft, claimed Shelley, and that he himself, by living in sin with his daughters, was rectifying the imbalance caused by it. Shelley writes as if he was convinced by his own arguments, but it is difficult for the outsider to see it as anything other than pure selfishness.

By now Mary knew that she too was in the family way. Only a handful of their former friends bothered to visit Shelley and his ladies. Thomas Hogg was one; Thomas Love Peacock was another. Charles Clairmont and Fanny Imlay, Mary's and Jane's brother and sister, paid furtive visits when they thought their parents wouldn't notice. Charles would give them small amounts of money for their everyday living expenses but he didn't have the funds to bail them out of the deep debt that Shelley was in. The bailiffs assailed them from time to time, causing Shelley to run off until things had settled. On Sundays he could return home because the bailiffs were not allowed to ply their trade on the Lord's Day.

Mary was not well throughout the pregnancy. Shelley advocated a strict vegetarian diet, and not a sound one at that. There are thoughts about this contributing to the unwellness of both Shelley and Mary. Mary would retire to bed early leaving Jane and Shelley to spend a lot of time together in the evenings. Mary was not happy about this, she didn't trust her sister and may not have trusted her lover either; she had, after all, witnessed what he did to his pregnant wife. Mary's solution to the problem was to suggest that Jane move out. The problem was that there was nowhere for her to go. She was not allowed to return home to Skinner Street, she had no other relatives willing to take her in, and Shelley had no money to find her separate lodgings; Mary was stuck with her.

Then, at the beginning of 1815, Jane did one of her extraordinary things that confounded everybody: she changed her name from Jane to Clara and then to Claire. With the change of name came a change of character. Instead of whingeing and blaming Shelley and her sister for their misery, Claire became animated and interested in things intellectual. She and Shelley began to go out and about, talking and walking, with she hanging on his every word. The strategy had the desired effect, and while Shelley began to enjoy Claire's company, Mary's jealousy became even more noticeable.

The little group were isolated socially and economically. It was frustrating but it also offered the opportunity Shelley had been looking for to put some of his free-love theories into practice. Here was a ready-made community of like-minded people who could participate in the experiment of their own will. While no one would be forced to sleep with or take up with another of the party if they didn't want to, there was no one to object to it if they did. With this in mind, Shelley encouraged Hogg, a frequent visitor, to declare his admiration of Mary. Shelley even went as far as inviting Hogg to visit Mary while he and Claire were deliberately out walking. Mary was not that impressed by Hogg's letter declaring undying love, although she suggested in a return letter that it was not something she would rule out altogether. They were not, she explained, well enough acquainted for them to become lovers (although she didn't put it as baldly as that), but she thought with time they might well be. Mary was bored. She was bored with being pregnant and left at home all the time while her lover and her sister enjoyed gadding about town. It was Shelley she wanted, not Hogg. When her boredom and sense of abandonment became too much Mary wrote to Hogg again suggesting that she was getting a bit more interested. However, it was Hogg who began to get cold feet over the affair. Meanwhile,

Shelley was enjoying overseeing Claire's education. She was to study languages, philosophy and poetry but she was to give up music. Claire obediently did as she was asked to do.

Towards the end of February 1815, Mary Godwin gave birth to a baby girl. The infant was sickly and was not expected to live beyond a day. She was never given a name and she died about ten days later. Mary was devastated; all that time waiting and fearing her lover would leave her and then her baby was gone. She went into a depression. It was faithful Fanny who came and nursed Mary, trying to console her. Hogg withdrew his attentions altogether, it was neither the time nor the place. Claire was still being blamed by Mary for trying to steal Shelley and Mary kept insisting that they find a new home for her.

Shelley approached Harriet again for more money but did not receive any. He asked Hogg for money and received a small amount. Finally Shelley went to his father and managed to get enough to cover all immediate debts and to provide for the near future. He was to get an annual allowance of £1,000, of which he would send one-fifth to Harriet in the form of maintenance. This windfall meant that Claire could be sent away. Mary had Shelley send her as far as Lynmouth, a small and relatively isolated place. They had spent a happy time there but it held nothing of interest for Claire nor any other prospects, such as marriage.

With Claire taken care of, Mary and Shelley were able to settle down together in Windsor. Mary was soon pregnant again. Seeing such domestic bliss and how conducive it was to Shelley's writing, Thomas Love Peacock conceded that Mary was a far more suitable partner for his friend than Harriet had been. He still did not condone the shabby treatment of Harriet by Shelley but he was happy to see some kind of settling down and contentment.

Claire, however, left on her own in a hostile place, was not going to let herself be tossed aside. She soon managed to make her way back to Shelley and Mary's house. Mary now had a baby boy, William, and Claire convinced her she could help to look after him. Perhaps she did and perhaps she didn't: the outcome was that Mary was as adamant not to live with Claire as she had been before. Thus Claire was set up in her own lodgings in town.

In 1816 Claire wrote a passionate letter to the poet Byron, offering herself to him. What possessed her, no one knows. Maybe she wanted a poet of her own, one even more famous than her sister's. Byron lived to regret inviting the young lady into his home, but he did so and they began an affair. To Claire it was a grand passion to rival Mary's with Shelley; to Byron it was a fling with a female slightly more elevated than a prostitute. Byron was already a married man, although he was certainly not a faithful one. When he tired of Claire he dumped her. However, Claire was not going to be discarded so thoughtlessly and she pursued him.

When she heard Byron was set to travel to Switzerland Claire put it to Shelley and Mary that they all three go there too, to recapture their first time away together. Shelley was enthusiastic; he wanted to meet Byron in person, the poet he admired so much and whose stature was already great. Mary was not going to let Shelley out of her sight, of course, so they took themselves off to Switzerland, a little older and wiser the second time around.

They set themselves up in the Hotel d'Angleterre and waited Byron's arrival. Within ten days he too was settled at the hotel. Claire sent a letter to him straightaway telling him that she was there too and available for his pleasure. No reply was made.

Shelley was in heaven. He and Byron, after their introduction, were getting on like a house on fire. They could talk poetry, philosophy and boating. There were days of walking, sailing and talking, endlessly. Byron moved into a villa beside the lake and the Shelleys moved into one not more than ten minutes away. The parties met nearly every day. Claire managed to reignite Byron's interest, although for him it was purely sexual. He is supposed to have told a friend that with a young girl throwing herself at him what else was he to do?

The weather turned bad, as it was want to do, and the friends were forced to spend long periods of time together indoors. It was one such occasion that led to the famous challenge that everyone should think up a ghost story. Mary, claiming she couldn't think of one, then had a vision one night that led to the writing of *Frankenstein*. Later, Shelley helped her with its composition. He suggested plot changes and edited the story for her; when they were back in England he also arranged for a publisher to publish it. Byron told Shelley how much he admired Mary; Claire was not mentioned and felt left out yet again. Unfortunately it turned out that she was pregnant with Byron's child. She confided in Shelley and Mary, and Shelley agreed to talk to his friend about it to find out what should happen with the child. Byron was not impressed, not even interested. He agreed that he would accept the child when it could leave its mother and that Claire could see the child whenever she wanted. At the time this declaration was made Claire seemed somewhat satisfied. Byron saw her as a common tart who had thrown herself at him until he finally responded – and who then wouldn't leave him alone. He considered her far beneath him, both socially and intellectually.

After the Claire and Byron episode the friendship between the two groups cooled considerably. Shelley was not sure he liked Byron the man as much as he admired his poetry (is it possible he felt a pang of guilt in recognising his own behaviour towards Harriet in Byron's for Claire). Shelley, Mary, their son William, and Claire returned to England. They settled for a time in Bath. Shelley commuted between there and London on writing and publishing business; Mary was engrossed in her novel and Claire, as usual, was feeling unwanted.

Out of the blue a letter arrived from Mary's half-sister Fanny. She was desperate, she felt she had been left to look after her parents all alone. She felt used and abandoned; she threatened to kill herself. Shelley set out to find her and rescue her but he was too late. She had already taken an overdose of laudanum. It was shocking for everyone, no one expected such an outburst from Fanny or that she would act on her threat. She was buried in an unmarked grave.

Mary threw herself deeply into working on *Frankenstein* to help alleviate the pain and guilt caused by Fanny's death. Claire wandered around bored and listless with pregnancy. In her own desperation Claire wrote to Byron, who eventually asked Shelley to tell her to stop pestering him. Then came the news that Harriet's pregnant and partly decomposed corpse was found in the Serpentine in Hyde Park. She had left a suicide note that pleaded with Shelley to let the children stay with her sister Eliza, but if he were to take their son then he was to be kind to him. Shelley immediately reacted by going to the sister's house and demanding custody of his children. If Harriet had not begged him to leave them with Eliza, whom he

Byron

detested, then maybe he wouldn't have considered uprooting them; more mouths to feed, more responsibility. But to be urged to leave them with the woman he hated was asking too much. Eliza would not let him in the house and refused to give up the children. Shelley threatened legal action, which he began to organise straightaway.

Harriet had been desperate. She loved her children but having been left by Shelley she had no future ahead of her. She could not marry again; she had to be dependent on her father (although Shelley eventually provided a £200 annual pension). She was shamed, lonely and, surprisingly, pregnant at the time of her death. It is now believed that the father of her unborn baby was Lieutenant Colonel Christopher Maxwell, who at the time of Harriet's death was overseas. The story goes that his landlady refused to pass on his letters to Harriet because she knew it was an adulterous affair. Harriet believed she had been abandoned once more and could not stand the thought of it. It is pretty safe to say it was not Shelley's child.

The only good thing that Harriet's death brought about was that it meant Shelley and Mary could get married; an odd step for two people so adamant that they didn't believe in the institution. Marry they did in a very quiet ceremony at the very end of December 1816. For his part, Shelley hoped that being married to his former mistress would help him get custody of his children by Harriet. Mary, although she may not have wanted to admit it, really wanted the stability of a monogamous relationship made with a legal procedure. With the marriage came permission to re-enter her father's household. Shelley was able to purchase the lease on a house in Marlow and in January 1817 Claire had a baby girl whom she called Alba. At least with the arrival of baby Alba Claire seemed to settle down into the role of perfectly satisfied motherhood. For Shelley it was not such a good start to the year, as he lost his case for custody of his children. They were taken from Eliza and their grandfather and put into the care of a neutral party. Shelley didn't see them again, although he was by law made to pay a regular amount for their care and upbringing.

Claire's baby was followed by Mary's whom they named Clara. Mary had finished her novel and Shelley had secured its publication. They had by this time settled into a fairly comfortable domestic group. It was only spoiled by Byron writing to demand his daughter be delivered to him in Italy. It upset them all. Claire was desperate to keep her beloved child; Shelley thought Byron a heartless brute and Mary did not see how a child as young as Alba could be sent all the way to Italy without people who loved her by her side. They planned and unplanned to take the child to Byron themselves. Also, by this time, Byron had insisted the girl be renamed Allegra.

The trip was finally settled and in 1818 the trio with three children went to Italy. Unfortunately little Clara Shelley, only a baby, came down with typhus and died. The Shelleys were left with little William, the son and heir. About nine months later he too got ill and died, he was only 3 years old. As seemed to be Mary's way, she conceived another child after the death of little Clara; the baby was born after the death of his older brother. This child was named after his father, Percy, and Florence because that was the place of his birth. Percy Florence lived to old age, inheriting his father's estates, though he was himself childless.

Allegra was duly delivered to Byron and Claire never saw her little girl again. Byron did not really want the bother of a child and when the little girl began to make demands on his time he had her given to the British-Consul General and his wife to look after. They were not too keen to have a man's illegitimate child thrust upon them, and when they left Venice, Allegra was passed on to the Danish Consul and his wife. Finally the child, age 4, was sent to a convent in Ravenna where she died quite suddenly in 1822 of a 'convulsive catarrhal attack' thought to be either a form of typhus or recurring malaria; she was just 5 years old.

Shelley never forgave Byron for his callous disregard for the little girl who was taken from her mother as a form of punishment and no other reason. Even though he had abandoned a wife and two children himself, Shelley may have learnt the preciousness of what he had lost. Certainly he couldn't understand why someone would act in the way Byron had done.

Claire finally settled down after the initial shock of her daughter's death. She wanted to return to Florence, where she had been making her own life for once, but the Shelleys were organising for her to go to Lerici with Mary, who was pregnant for a fifth time. Claire did not really have a choice; she was still dependent on the Shelleys for her maintenance. It was probably just as well that she did go with them as Mary suffered a terrible miscarriage, bleeding so profusely that she could easily have died. Shelley was full of the fact that he had ordered his wife to be placed in a tub of ice to stem the blood flow, but it was most likely Claire who gave the emotional support Mary needed. A month later Mary Shelley was to become a widow. Her husband, his friend Edward Williams and a young Englishman, 18-year-old Charles Vivian, went out sailing and were caught in a storm. The boat went missing. Mary and Edward's wife Jane had no idea that anything had gone wrong until several days later when they had no word from their husbands. They both went down to Livorno, where the boat had been heading, to meet with Leigh Hunt and Byron, who also had no idea that anything was wrong. Nearly two weeks after Shelley and his friends went out in the boat their bodies were found washed up on the coast.

Mary reacted to her husband's death in a quiet and dignified manner that was thought cold by some of her friends. Claire was still with her for support, they had both loved Shelley in their own way. Now Mary had no income; she didn't know if Shelley's father would continue to pay the allowance he had granted his son. Mary was going to have to earn her living and, as far as she was concerned, so was Claire. The sisters' bond was broken at last.

Claire did not seem to resent the fact that Mary couldn't keep her. She took herself off to become a governess. Her first stop was to visit her brother Charles in Vienna. However, she felt unwelcome in Austria and when she was able to Claire took up a position with Countess Zotoff to educate her children in St Petersburg. Before she had left Italy Claire had found she was suddenly bombarded with offers of marriage and declarations of undying love from a number of different men of varying ages and incomes. She refused every one of them although she was penniless at the time. Perhaps, after being tied to her sister for so many years, Claire liked the idea of total independence and freedom from love and men. After spending time with the countess, Claire went further north into Russia, at which time none of the family heard from her for more than a year.

Mary stayed in Italy with the Hunt family, until she was encouraged by Byron to go back to England. She had decided to devote the rest of her life (she was sure she would die at the age of 36, like her mother) to putting Shelley's papers in order and trying to get his poems published. She would keep herself and Percy by writing. After all, she was the author of *Frankenstein* and another novel, *Valperga*. In August 1823 Mary Shelley and her 3-year-old son were back in England. She eventually managed to get a £200 loan from her father-in-law that would be paid back out of her old man's estate when he died.

Then suddenly Mary Shelley found she was a celebrity author herself. *Frankenstein* had been turned into a stage play and was drawing huge crowds. Her novel went into a second publication and her name became a household word. Thus Mary was able to devote much of her time on returning to England to editing Shelley's work and enhancing his reputation as a kind and gentle man.

Mary became a noted novelist in her own right and lived to see her only son, Percy Florence Shelley, inherit his grandfather's estates and marry a respectable widow of independent means, Jane Gibson St John. While the kindly Percy was happy to ramble about his estates, his wife was keen to secure the Shelley, Godwin, Wollstonecraft legacy and helped her mother-in-law with Shelley's papers. Mary lived well beyond her self-predicted 36 years of age but she still died relatively young at 53 of a brain tumour.

Claire lived to be 80. She did not have an easy life after Shelley's death but she did maintain her new-found independence. She worked in Russia for several years, but always in fear of being discovered to have socially unacceptable relations. After Byron's death in 1824 Claire was anxious that one of the many biographies coming out about him would reveal her part in his life. Eventually word did get out and she then found it hard to get employment. She struggled on for twenty years working as a governess with one family or another.

In 1846 Shelley's father finally died and Shelley's kind legacy to Claire was made available to her. It meant she could give up teaching. She retired to Florence and spent much of her old age making sure that the facts about her youth shared with Shelley, Byron, Mary and other famous people was not mistold. She did claim, outrageously, that Byron had only pretended their daughter had died in order to upset her – and had sent the body of a goat in the coffin to England, not that of a child.

Claire Clairmont died in 1879.

Part 5
Mistress as Muse

Throughout the world and throughout time artists have found the need for inspiration to help them achieve their greatest works. Artists today may well tell you that hard work is an excellent form of inspiration and that you need to grab it by the throat not wait for it to float down from on high. It is true though that artists, whether they are musicians, painters or writers, do respond better to certain stimuli over others. The traditional source of inspiration is the beautiful woman, particularly for visual artists. It has been such a constant source of artistic expression that Greek mythology named it in terms of goddesses: the Muses. The word muse has stuck and a human female will sometimes captivate an artist to such an extent that the creative juices cannot flow without it.

ELLEN 'NELLY' LAWLESS TERNAN
THE INVISIBLE MISTRESS
OF CHARLES DICKENS

Charles Dickens is a name everyone knows. His stories are admired the world over, as much today as they were in his own time. There has never been any doubt that he had a vivid imagination, boundless creative energy and was a character fit for one of his own novels (and indeed several of his books had strong autobiographical elements). He was married for many years to Catherine (*née* Hogarth), with whom he had ten children. Dickens built up a reputation as being a family man and that children and loyalty in marriage were very important. And for a long time they were, until Charles Dickens, at the age of 45, fell desperately in love with a young woman who was roughly the same age as one of his daughters. Infatuation made Dickens become ruthlessly cruel to his faithful wife and extremely secretive about his love for the young woman. Although Dickens was adamant he was not having an affair with another woman he couldn't help himself from dropping huge incriminating hints about it. He knew that if word got out that he had taken a mistress it could devastate his reputation and his livelihood.

Dickens was in his mid-40s at the time of writing *The Frozen Deep* and was beginning to find his long-time marriage to Catherine uninspiring. Catherine, after so many years of childbearing, was growing stout and homely.

Who was this mysterious young woman? In 1857 Dickens engaged a number of professional actors to perform *The Frozen Deep* with him, a play that he had helped co-author with his friend Wilkie Collins. Among the thespians were a well-known but semi-retired actress and two of her daughters. It was one of these two young ladies who caught Dickens's attention and ultimately stole his heart.

When Dickens had been a teenager himself he had fallen deeply in love with an intoxicatingly pretty young woman called Maria Beadnell. For a long time after Dickens's death nothing was really publicly known about Maria and her part in the young Dickens's life. Just after the turn of the twentieth century an American collector of curios, Mr William K. Bixby, came across a bundle of letters containing Dickens's signature. The bundle turned out to contain two lots of letters to the one woman, but years apart. The first group were letters by a teenage Dickens to a young lady named Maria Beadnell, the second group were to the same lady but to her married, middle-aged self Maria Winter.

The letters could not be published in Britain at that time because of the copyright laws. Mr Bixby took the letters home across the Atlantic and handed them over to the Bibliophile Society to have 493 copies of them made, all to contain the society's book-plate. These were to be distributed to members of the society. Several other copies were made and these were placed in the Congress Library in Washington.

The bulk of the early letters show Dickens as a would-be suitor pouring his heart out to Miss Maria Beadnell. For a while Maria seemed to enjoy his attention and encouraged him. After a stint abroad, however, Maria spurned Dickens and broke his heart. Maria became the inspiration for the delicate, impractical and demanding character of Dora, who becomes the needy wife of David Copperfield in the novel of the same name. Maria Beadnell may well have been the author's first muse. The second bundle of letters were written after Dickens and a married Maria Winter made contact again some twenty years later.

In 1836 Dickens married the much more sensible Catherine Hogarth. They began life together with Catherine's younger sister Mary coming to live with them. The following year Dickens held Mary in his arms as she was dying. He had idolised her. The depth of Dickens's mourning led to him taking a ring from her dead finger and wearing it on one of his own for the rest of his life, keeping a bundle of her clothes and letting her spirit enter a number of his poignant characters: little Nell being among the most obvious. Mary Hogarth, with her youthful freshness and vivacity, her imagination and willingness to be entranced by her brother-in-law's stories and wit, was the perfect muse for the writer, especially as she was never to grow old.

In 1842 Mary Hogarth was replaced by another of Catherine's sisters, Georgina. She too came to live with the Dickens family when she was 16. This was the year that Charles and Catherine went to the United States for Dickens's first lecture tour. Georgina was left at home to look after the couple's four children. In 1843 Dickens wrote a letter to his mother-in-law asserting that Georgina was the spirit of Mary returned to them. Georgina became the new muse in Dickens's life. Perhaps, as Georgina passed into mature womanhood, although she didn't grow matronly as her older sister did, she nevertheless lost some of her angelic loveliness.

In 1855 Maria Beadnell resurfaced in Dickens's life. She wrote him a letter, and he enthusiastically responded. They exchanged a

Charles Dickens

number of letters talking about their youthful friendship, Dickens certainly implying that he had deeply loved her. Maria answered that she too had been in love with him but that she had been prevented from following her passion by her family. The brief correspondence led to a meeting, what was probably going to be a secret assignation in Dickens's mind, between himself and his first true love. To be fair, Maria had warned him that she was no longer the slim beauty he had known over twenty years ago. Dickens was not going to be put off by what surely must be modesty. Yet he was in for a shock. Maria, nearly 45, was indeed a portly, middle-aged woman. Dickens did not try to conceal his disappointment. Maria, hoping that there might yet be an old spark to reignite the amorous flame, continued writing to him but Dickens's replies grew cold and he evaded making a commitment to seeing her again. Instead he immortalised the older Maria in the form of Flora Finching in *Little Dorrit*, just as he had done her young self in *David Copperfield*. Another muse had bitten the dust.

By the time Dickens met Ellen Ternan he was again in need of that sweet, adolescent muse that could help stimulate memories of Mary Hogarth.

Ellen 'Nelly' Ternan (1839–1914) was born in Rochester, Kent into a theatrical family, the youngest of three girls. There had been a brother but he had died as a baby. Ellen's mother, Frances Ternan, *née* Jarman, had played with such notable actors as Edmund Kean and Charles Kemble. Thomas Ternan, Nelly's father, had died in 1846, with hardly a penny to his name. The bereft family came under the protection of William Charles Macready, a long time friend of Dickens.

When Dickens met Nelly, she had been acting for some fifteen years already. She and her sisters had been introduced to the stage in their early childhood and had been presented as an 'infant phenomena'. Maria, the sister next to Nelly in age, was showing great promise in comedy theatre and singing. Fanny, the eldest of the girls, was playing Oberon in a production of a *Midsummer Night's Dream* at the Princess Theatre at the time Dickens engaged the rest of the family to play in *The Frozen Deep* for a performance at the Manchester Free Trade Hall. Nelly had just finished playing her first adult role on stage, that of Hippomenes in a satire by Frank Talfourd at the Haymarket Theatre. Nelly had found it difficult to shake off

Ellen 'Nelly' Lawless Ternan

the reputation of herself as a child prodigy and the recurring roles that this offered.

The Frozen Deep was inspired by reports by the Scottish surveyor John Rae, of evidence of cannibalism among the members of the Arctic expedition of Sir Charles Franklin that had left England in 1845 never to return. The play was an allegorical denial of this supposed barbaric fate. Dickens had started helping Wilkie Collins to write the play in 1856, at least he maintained that he was just altering a line or two here and there, though in reality a fair bit of it is the work of Dickens and not Collins. Dickens was outraged at the suggestion that Franklin and his men would resort to something as barbaric, as un-English as eating one another, no matter if they were starving.

Frances Ternan played Nurse Esther, Maria had the main female role of Clara Burnham and Nelly was given a minor part as Lucy Crayford. The cast was initially gathered together for three days of intensive rehearsals in Dickens's own home, Tavistock House. From there they travelled as a company, taking the train to Manchester and boarding at the same hotel.

The little company gave three performances of the play at the Free Trade Hall in Manchester, the proceeds from ticket sales going directly into a charitable fund to aid the widow and family of Dickens's long-time friend Douglas Jerrold. The event raised £2,000 (around £117,000 today) and brought the audience to a torrent of tears. Dickens was elated by his success (not only with the play but with his own performance).

However, after the adrenalin rush from the play's triumph, Dickens began to display a restlessness unlike any he had previously shown. It manifested itself with the need, as he suggested himself, to climb high mountains. Surely this was a strong symptom of being hopelessly in love.

It was unclear for some time as to which of the two Ternan sisters was the object of his desire, until he wrote of little lilac gloves and golden hair: Nelly was the blonde. Dickens felt he had found his muse in the young woman, only a little older than his own daughter Katie. The more he seemed to think about Nelly the more he seemed displeased with his frumpy old wife. Catherine took the blame for all her husband's unhappiness; she was unimaginative, she had no creativity, she didn't understand his needs.

Dickens tried to allay some of his restlessness by going on a walking tour with his friend Wilkie Collins; their adventures would be written up in *Household Words* in a piece called 'The Lazy Tour of Two Idle Apprentices'. While he was away Dickens wrote only to his sister-in-law Georgina and not at all to his wife, which was rather unusual in itself. He ignored Catherine entirely in his letters to her sister, although he sent his love to all the children. When the walking tour was over (ending with Collins falling over and spraining his ankle) the pair travelled straight to the races at Doncaster where Dickens had already booked them accommodation. Coincidentally, the Ternan girls were going to be there and he couldn't help but bump into them.

Nelly and Maria were performing in a play in the town and Dickens went along to see them. He was outraged at the treatment the women were given by the audience and defended them fiercely. This was followed by a series of social outings, visiting local attractions, going to the races and showing off in front of the ladies.

At some point in the drama Catherine is supposed to have opened a parcel from her husband containing a bracelet. It was obviously not meant for her but for young Ellen 'Nelly' Ternan – and poor Catherine knew it. When Dickens was confronted with his wife's suspicions, that he was having an extramarital affair, and with a girl young enough to be his daughter, Dickens was most self-righteous and claimed that he had no designs on the purity of the girl. Perhaps there was something in this. Maybe there was no sexual relationship between Dickens and Nelly Ternan. Perhaps Dickens really did require a girl of virginal beauty to stimulate his creativity, as his own sweet Mary Hogarth had, as had the youthful Maria Beadnell and the ever faithful but now mature Georgina Hogarth. All this is speculation, however, and it may be that any proof of a more physical relationship has been lost in the dozens of letters destroyed by both Dickens and Nelly.

Another source claims that the bracelet was actually a pendant with a portrait of Dickens in it, given by him to Nelly. It came to Catherine's notice when the item came back from the jewellers where it had been repaired. According to the same source, it was a jealous Georgina

Hogarth who opened the parcel and told her sister about it. Catherine is supposed to have attacked her husband with her brush and comb.

In December 1857 Dickens had his dressing room – adjoined to the bedroom he had for so many years shared with Catherine – turned into a small bedroom for himself. The door between the two rooms was sealed up. Catherine was told none of this directly. It was almost the end of the marriage. Catherine was to receive one more housekeeping cheque and that would be it. In Dickens's mind, he was free to follow the passion of his heart and to begin his financial support of Nelly. Initially it began in subtle ways such as buying her a performance engagement with a theatre at the Haymarket. Dickens confessed to J.B. Buckstone, manager of the theatre, that this would not be the last of his interest in the young lady.

Dickens and Catherine's marriage came to its absolute end about three months later. Dickens had tried to come to an amicable arrangement with Catherine, or at least he pretended it was. He first suggested that they cohabit at Tavistock House with her keeping out of his way during the daytime but continuing to act as hostess to his friends and business guests. When this was not acceptable Dickens suggested Catherine move into the flat at Gad's Hill with a single servant; he would stay in the family residence with the children and be looked after by Georgina, Catherine's younger sister.

Catherine stood her ground and refused to be humiliated by her husband. In the end they settled for a formal separation. Dickens unkindly claimed that Catherine was suffering inexplicable and outrageous jealousy and that she was apt to imagine things.

To add insult to injury Dickens also kept asserting that Catherine had been and was still incapable of normal maternal feelings for her children and that she had never loved them or cared for them as she should. The list of complaints against poor Catherine grew with the business of separation. He said she was begging to be released from her unhappy marriage and that she knew she had been unfair to her husband. He said outright that she suffered from delusions, and even went as far as pretending, for the benefit of any visitor to the house, that she loved and played with her children.

At the same time his infatuation for Nelly became more intense; although Dickens tried hard to keep it out of the public eye he could not help dropping hints all over the place that he was very interested in some beautiful young creature. What Nelly thought at the time is not known, as all correspondence between herself and Dickens was deliberately destroyed, as was his wish on his deathbed.

In 1860 Dickens supplied the financial means for the Ternan family to take out a lease on a not insubstantial house in Houghton Place; the lease was put into Nelly's own name on her twenty-first birthday that same year. It was here that Dickens was a regular visitor. Dickens would take Nelly Ternan and Georgina Hogarth, who had remained part of his household when he and Catherine split up, to social events in London, not seeming to be worried that they were all three seen in public together.

In 1861, having sold Tavistock House, Dickens rented a place in the vicinity of the Ternan residence so that he could visit often. He not only made sure the Ternan family had all they needed for a respectable and comfortable life but he also helped Fanny, the eldest daughter, to go abroad to study. He saw himself as the benefactor to a family of talented and deserving young women, in this way always justifying his attentions to the family to his friends.

Nelly Ternan did at some stage become the kept woman in Charles Dickens's later life. She gave up her acting career and lived in one or other of the places he rented under a false name. At one time it is thought that Nelly and her mother were living in Condette in France, as at one time Dickens was making numerous trips to the Continent with unexplained absences from legitimate activities.

About 1863 Charles was offered a lucrative deal to take a six-month tour of Australia, sponsored by a Melbourne catering company. It would have drawn in an immense £10,000 (around £585,000 today) but would have meant half a year away from his beloved. Dickens did not take the offer.

There is no evidence left as to the absolute nature of the relationship between Dickens and Nelly Ternan. One of Dickens's daughters was sure that an illegitimate child had been born to them, but who died in infancy. Yet nothing has been recorded of this possibility.

Then in 1865, on Friday 9 June, Dickens was travelling on a train with Nelly and another woman, who was probably her mother, when the train crashed off a bridge. Dickens was busy helping the injured but he made sure his companions, who remained nameless, were safely put into care. Dickens had been afraid that he may be called as a witness at the inquest to the crash and that it would come out that he had been travelling with Nelly. However, he did not have to appear at the inquest and was able to keep Nelly's name out of the press.

After Dickens's death Nelly confessed to the Revd William Benham that she was ashamed of the affair she'd had with Dickens, implying that it had involved sexual intimacy but not openly declaring so. It may be that she felt guilty about being the catalyst that split Dickens from his wife and then accepted the man's financial support, or that she was in all ways Dickens's mistress and that this was the intimacy she spoke of to the Revd Benham. She told him that the feelings of regret at having been Dickens's companion had intruded upon their life together and that her own guilt had brought unhappiness to both of them.

Ellen 'Nelly' Ternan was left a lifelong legacy by Dickens in his will. It was enough to make her independent and comfortable. At age 37 – but obviously retaining her youthful beauty because she was able to pretend she was only 24 – Nelly Ternan married George Wharton Robinson, aged 26. Nelly's sister Maria was instrumental in introducing the couple at a party in Oxford where George was a recent graduate. They set up a boys' school in Margate and had two children together, a boy, Geoffrey, and a girl, Gladys. When George was ill in 1886 they sold their school. Life was financially difficult as Mrs Robinson, especially after the school had gone. Both Nelly and George took on teaching commitments and also ran an unsuccessful market garden for a short time. George died in 1910. Nelly went to live with her eldest sister Frances but died only four years later of cancer.

When the couple's son, Geoffrey, returned home from having fought in the First World War, he was able to look into his family documents. He discovered that his mother had lied about her age and that she had been an actress, along with her sisters and mother. During an interview with Henry Dickens after some of the findings, Geoffrey was shocked to learn about his late mother's relationship with Charles Dickens and possibly about the birth of an illegitimate child. Geoffrey burnt all the documents he had received on his mother's death and apparently never spoke of her again.

THE TWO WOMEN IN THE LIFE OF WILKIE COLLINS

Wilkie Collins was a close long-time friend of Charles Dickens. He witnessed the breakdown of the Dickenses' marriage, knew about his passion for the lovely young Ellen 'Nelly' Ternan, and became, through the marriage of Dickens's daughter Katie to Collins's brother Charles, a sort of relation. Collins didn't judge his friend on the matter of his affair of the heart, although when being sounded out by Dickens on the matter he did advise him to leave love well alone: falling in love was not the problem but what was to be done when one fell out of it again.

At the time of Dickens's emerging passion for Ellen 'Nelly' Ternan, about the time of their 'Lazy Walking Tour', Collins had not yet met the woman who was to live with him for almost the rest of his life.

CAROLINE GRAVES

Caroline Graves (c.1830–95) was and is still very much a mystery. When she came into Collins's life she told him she was much younger than she really was, a lie that she perpetuated for a very long time. She also made out that she was born into a gentleman's family and that her husband, supposedly dead, had been of independent means. She did not even go by her christened name, Elizabeth, but called herself Caroline (this may have been a second name, which would not be unusual to use as her preferred name). When, or if, Caroline revealed the truth about herself is unknown.

There is a fanciful story told by the painter John Everett Millais to his son telling how Collins first met Caroline Graves and how it inspired the novel *A Woman in White*. Collins and his brother lived together at Hanover Terrace. Millais had dined with them and then the three men had wandered back to Millais's studio in Gower

Street. They were near to Finchley Road when they were startled by an anguished cry coming from a nearby garden. Before any of them could respond, the garden gate was flung open and a beautiful young woman dressed in flowing white garments became illuminated in the moonlight. She looked towards the men as if begging for help but then turned and fled down the street. Only Collins followed her, and wasn't seen again by his friend or family that night.

This story fits in wonderfully as a tale of artistic inspiration but it is doubtful as to whether all the details are accurate. It is suspected that the story had been heavily embroidered by Millais for the amusement of his son.

It is thought that the woman was Caroline Graves and that she had been held prisoner in the house for several months. This story came from the lips of Kate Perugini (formerly Collins's sister-in-law) when she recounted it to Gladys Storey for her book *Dickens and Daughter*. It was not known if the captor was the woman's husband or some other man, nor where her young daughter was at the time.

Other sources suggest that Caroline, a widow, met Collins when she lived with her widowed mother-in-law near Collins's lodgings in Howland Street. This is certainly a less dramatic story than the previous one and, therefore, may well be the true one. And, according to the same source, Collins did not settle down to live with Caroline until he was financially stable.

Caroline began to live with Collins probably around 1858. She claimed she was a widow, her husband having died in 1852, but there seems to be some doubt about this as well. It also turned out that her father was not a gentleman named Courtney but a carpenter called John Compton, her mother his wife Sarah. Her husband, George Graves, whom she married in Bath in 1850, was not a man of independent income but a hard-working shorthand writer who was the son of a stonemason. These were humble roots indeed. The couple had a daughter, Elizabeth, who went to live with her mother and Collins.

Whatever Caroline's history really was she certainly gave Collins a comfortable home both physically and emotionally. What would have sealed Caroline's happiness with Collins would have been marriage, but that was one thing he always denied her. Ten years after they first met Caroline suddenly left Collins to marry a man called Joseph Clow. Collins made no objections and even went to the wedding. The marriage was over in two years or less and Caroline returned to her home with Collins as if nothing had changed.

Because of her situation as a kept woman, Caroline could not entertain publicly for her lover's guests unless they were among his close friends, neither could she attend public functions with him. For the sake of propriety, Collins told people she was his housekeeper. However, Caroline was able to travel abroad with Collins as no one would know the true nature of their relationship. She was devoted to Collins, despite his refusing to marry her and the fact that he was keeping a much younger woman, Martha Rudd and their three children, not far away. She nursed him when he was ill, which happened frequently, often seeing to his business and correspondence on his behalf. In his final illness she was his constant companion and nurse. She was with him when he died in 1889.

MARTHA RUDD

Unlike her rival Caroline Graves, Martha Rudd (1845–1919) did nothing to hide her even humbler origins. She was the daughter of a shepherd, James Rudd and his wife Mary (*née* Andrew), and had four brothers and three sisters.

In 1861 Martha and her sister Alice were working as domestic servants for an innkeeper in Yarmouth. It was there that she probably met Collins, who was staying at the coast while he did research for his novel *Armadale* in 1864. Collins, at 40, was twice her age.

It wasn't until 1868 that it was known that Collins had moved his much younger second mistress into a house at 33 Bolsover Street. The following year Martha gave birth to their first child, a girl they called Marian. She was followed by another daughter, Harriet, two years later and finally by a boy, William, in 1874. Only William's birth is registered as the two girls were born before it became the law to register births.

Martha and her children were set up comfortably but not lavishly in a house not too far from Collins's dwelling with Caroline. The children visited their father and his first mistress at his house, but it is unlikely that Martha ever set foot there. Martha was also never given the opportunity to socialise with Collins and did not even get to travel on the Continent with him. She did receive a handsome allowance though.

When Collins died it was not considered seemly for Martha and the children to attend the funeral. They had a wreath sent to his other house. Caroline did attend the funeral, but this meant that people of higher social standing could not as they would be tainted by having been received by Collins's long-time mistress. Lady Millais, among others, sent an empty coach as a mark of respect. When Caroline died, six years after Collins, Martha took over the job of attending the grave in which Caroline was also laid to rest.

THE PRE-RAPHAELITE BROTHERHOOD

Is there a more clichéd subject than the painter falling in love with his model? Usually the model is young, female and often nude or draped in alluring fabric. The more the painter concentrates on getting right the form, the atmosphere and the essence of the subject, the more the bond might be strengthened. At least this would be the romantic ideal of a nineteenth-century male painter and his female model. For the Pre-Raphaelite Brotherhood the ethereal beauty of the model was of utmost importance; she needed the look.

The Pre-Raphaelite Brotherhood was founded in 1848 by three earnest young artists: William Holman Hunt, John Everett Millais and Dante Gabriel Rossetti. Later, four more members joined the brotherhood: William Michael Rossetti (Dante's brother), James Collinson, Frederic George Stephens and Thomas Woolner.

The inspiration for the art produced by these men was the art, poetry and stories that came before Raphael, the great Italian painter:

medieval manuscripts, Arthurian legends, and tragic, romantic tales of lost love. The colours were rich and bright and nature was to be observed closely. And there was a particular type of beauty that nearly all the men admired.

Models were discovered, shared, fallen in love with, made mistresses, married, and became the mistresses of another. The stories of the women involved with the Pre-Raphaelites are so intertwined that it can be difficult to find where one affair begins and another ends.

Let's begin with the one model who was the closest to providing this standard: Elizabeth Siddal.

Elizabeth Siddal was born on 25 July 1829 to a maker of cutlery, Charles Crooke Siddal and his wife, Eleanor (*née* Evans). This was a respectable lower-middle-class family and Elizabeth was brought up to be literate, good and useful. She was expected to earn a living in her teens until she married into her own class, perhaps a craftsman or business owner like her father. Whether Lizzie would have followed this conventional path if she hadn't been snapped up by the Pre-Raphaelite fraternity is debatable. Lizzie was already a great reader of poetry, having discovered a poem by Tennyson on a fragment of newspaper used to wrap the butter. It is said to have inspired the girl to begin writing her own. For a cutlery-maker's daughter this was rather ominous.

Lizzie was always a pale-skinned girl, slim and with masses of bushy red hair. Her eyes were large and heavy lidded, giving her an other-worldly look. A painter associated with the brotherhood, Walter Deverell, discovered Lizzie working as a milliner. At first Deverell kept his find to himself, but as he needed to show off his work it was inevitable that Miss Siddal would become known to the other painters in the circle.

Lizzie was taken on as a model by a small number of painters on the understanding that she could keep working part-time at the hat shop. Modelling won out in the end and Lizzie became the face of Pre-Raphaelitism. The downside of being an artist's model was some of the outrageous things one had to do. John Everett Millais decided to use Lizzie as his model for the drowning Ophelia. He filled a bathtub with water, under which he placed lamps to keep the water warm, then he bade Lizzie wear a medieval gown and lie down in the water, where he then strew flowers over her. He was a meticulous craftsman and took a long time to capture his subject to his standard of perfection. Sometimes, more often than not probably, the lamps went out and the water got cold, very cold. Lizzie got very sick. Her father was furious with the irresponsible artist and made him pay for Lizzie's medical expenses. However, it did not put Lizzie off from working with the Brotherhood again.

It wasn't long before Dante Gabriel Rossetti, named after the great medieval Italian poet Dante Alighieri, had Lizzie almost entirely to himself. She really did become his muse and over the years he constantly drew and painted her. Rossetti, probably inspired by his namesake, took Lizzie to be his Beatrice. In 1851 he declared his love for her and within the next twelve months the pair were living together. Rossetti was not married so living with Lizzie was not adultery, she was not 'the other woman' but was a kept woman, unmarried and living with the man to whom she was artistic muse. And Rossetti did still have sexual affairs with other women. Lizzie was referred to as his mistress because of the fact they weren't married. In 1853 the couple became engaged to be married, but for one reason or another Rossetti always put off the actual event. It was probably because he knew what his family's reaction to Lizzie would be. Lizzie herself thought that Rossetti was most likely on the hunt for a newer, younger model with whom to replace her.

While she was with Rossetti Lizzie was encouraged to paint, draw and write poetry, not only by Rossetti but also by the art critic John Ruskin, the poet Algernon Swinburne and others. At one point Ruskin was paying Lizzie £150 a year for the right to all her artwork.

For most of her adult life Lizzie suffered from mysterious health problems. For decades it was believed that she had tuberculosis but in the last few years of her life evidence has emerged that suggests she had some kind of intestinal disorder. Her friends packed her off to Paris and Nice for health treatments.

Finally, in 1860, Rossetti made the commitment and married Lizzie Siddal. Why he finally did so has been speculated by all and sundry. Rossetti may have married Lizzie out of a feeling of guilt for having not married her for so long; he may have married her in response to his one-time love, Jane Burden, marrying William Morris.

Elizabeth Siddal

On Wednesday 23 May 1860 they married in St Clements Church, Hastings, with two official witnesses but no friends or family.

The marriage did not mean a happy ending by any means. Lizzie continued to suffer from bad health and a feeling of insecurity. She had by this time also become addicted to laudanum, originally prescribed for pain reduction. Nevertheless, a joyous event was announced in 1861: Lizzie was pregnant. Although the pregnancy followed through to full term the baby girl was stillborn. Lizzie was grief-stricken; a year later Lizzie was dead too.

The night before Lizzie's death has had several different accounts recorded. Swinburne, one of Lizzie's admirers, says that there was a dinner at a restaurant, which the Rossettis both attended. Lizzie was lively, engaging and even happy; she was pregnant again. After the dinner Rossetti took his wife home, tucked her up in bed and went out again. When he returned at about midnight he found Lizzie unconscious but still alive in bed with an empty laudanum bottle beside it. Although attempts were made to revive her she died in the morning. Many years later Oscar Wilde put forth another version of the story. Lizzie was already doped up to the eyeballs on laudanum when she arrived at the restaurant. Her behaviour was wild, outrageous and embarrassing; Rossetti, humiliated and angry, took her home, put her in bed and threw the laudanum bottle at her telling her to take the lot. And then he went out.

Probably Rossetti, if he did taunt his sick wife, did so out of desperation and didn't mean or expect her to act on it. Perhaps it was an accidental overdose, just as the inquest found. Or it could have been the build-up of arsenic in her system through long-term use of Fowler's Solution, a popular medicine of the time, used for the improvement of the complexion. Rossetti was certainly wracked with guilt afterwards. This may have been because he wasn't actually at home when she took the overdose. It is commonly thought he was off visiting other lady friends or was at a brothel. Full of remorse and perhaps feeling poetically romantic at his loss, Rossetti put a bundle of his unpublished poems into the casket with Lizzie before it was buried. This was another thing for him to regret.

As with Dante Alighieri after the loss of his muse Beatrice, Rossetti flung himself into a fit of work churning out yet more drawings of his beloved Lizzie. Two years after her death Rossetti picked up the painting of *Beata Beatrix* he had begun before Lizzie died. He did not complete it until 1870. It shows Lizzie as Beatrice, already pale with death but sitting in a trance with closed eyes. A dove drops a poppy into her open hands, in the background love and Dante gaze at each other. This is the death of Beatrice as immortalised in Dante Aligh-ieri's poem *Vita Nuova*. For Rossetti, the scholar and painter, this was his own testament to his greatest muse. Certainly it is the sketches, drawings and paintings of Lizzie that have earned him his reputation as a painter, and it is these that have fetched the biggest prices after his death.

This brings us to the tale of the equally beautiful Jane Burden. Where Lizzie Siddal had been pale skinned with red hair, the idealised Celt, Jane, was dark haired and exotic looking. Jane was born in Oxford in 1839 to Robert Burden, a stable hand, and his wife Ann, a former domestic servant. Jane and her sister Bessie were probably destined for the same work as their mother, followed by marriage and children. In 1857 the two sisters went to a production put on by the Drury Lane Theatre Company in Oxford. It just happened that Dante Rossetti and one of the later Pre-Raphaelite painters, Edward Burne-Jones, were in Oxford painting an Arthurian-themed mural for the Oxford Union library. If they had not been in Oxford when Jane Burden went to the theatre, and if the men had not noticed her (although she was definitely eye-catching) then Jane Burden may well have had a completely different kind of life. Instead she was discovered as the next Pre-Raphaelite model and was whisked back to London with them.

Rossetti saw in Jane the antithesis of his ethereal Lizzie. Jane was dark where Lizzie was fair; Jane was the model for the likes of Guinevere, a fallen and treacherous woman whose beauty caused trouble, while Lizzie was forever the angelic Beatrice; Jane's beauty was sensuous and earthy where Lizzie's was fragile.

Jane, as the child of lower-class folk, was uneducated. Her mother was illiterate, although there is no mention of Jane having been so too. Jane was naturally intelligent, however, and a fast learner. The painters took it upon themselves to encourage her to read, learn and improve herself. She not only became a great reader but she also became fluent in French and Italian.

It was William Morris who ended up stealing Jane away as his bride, although he did not take her whole heart. They became engaged in 1858 and were married the following year in St Michael's Church, Oxford. There was a story circulating as to the effect that the marriage had on Rossetti. Some stated that it was because of the Morris-Burden match that Rossetti finally settled down properly with Lizzie Siddal; if he couldn't have Jane he'd better settle for his previous love. Others suggested that Jane had been asked by Rossetti to marry him but he felt he should stick with Lizzie.

After Jane's marriage she put a huge amount of effort into metamorphosing herself into a lady. She took up the piano and played it very well, she worked hard at losing her working-class accent and her manners. She may well have been the inspiration behind the character of Liza Higgins in Bernard Shaw's *Pygmalion*. Certainly in later years no one could have guessed at Jane Morris's humble background.

Jane bore William two daughters, Jane Alice and Mary. Her first child was born about the time Lizzie Siddal gave birth to her stillborn daughter. During the next decade Jane Morris became close to Rossetti; it is thought their affair started in 1865. Morris went off to Iceland for an extended study visit. While he was away Rossetti and Jane Morris became indisputable lovers. On Morris's return in 1871 he could not deny the fact that his wife was in love with his best friend and business partner. He was not in a position to make a fuss about the situation. Morris himself had been an advocate of free love and would not play the hypocrite. He stood by his wife and friend.

Jane's affair with Rossetti lasted until his death in 1882 although things had cooled considerably before the end, not least because Jane was put off by his addiction to chloral. Two years after Rossetti's death and two before Morris's, Jane met the poet and political activist Wilfrid Scawen Blunt and became his mistress until 1894.

Jane Morris was beautiful even in her older age. She died in January 1914. It is perhaps at this point that we should mention the curious case of John Ruskin, who was instrumental in promoting the work of the Pre-Raphaelite Brotherhood and, although never considered a great artist himself, was inspired by the beauty around him. He had an odd upbringing by his two domineering puritanical parents, who kept him tied to them for a great deal of his adult life. This may have been how everything fell into a mess on his domestic front.

Ruskin was introduced to 13-year-old Euphemia Gray about 1841, he was 22. Seven years later they married. Nothing appeared to be wrong until the wedding night, when Effie expected certain things to happen but they didn't. In fact Ruskin told Effie that nothing of a sexual nature ever would happen between them. Effie was puzzled and wondered what was so wrong with her that her husband didn't want to make love to her. Not only did Effie not have the pleasures of a normal married life she also had Ruskin's parents to put up with, who managed every part of the couple's lives.

The speculations abound surrounding Ruskin's inability to consummate his marriage to a beautiful woman. The obvious one is that Ruskin was not able to perform the deed. Another was that once seeing Effie's pubic hair he was so disgusted that he couldn't bring himself to touch her; there was no pubic hair on the classical statues he so adored. Another idea was that Ruskin felt that if he had sex with Effie they would both be besmirched with carnal sin – and how could he do that to such a pure creature as Effie?

In 1851 the Ruskins became friends with the painter John Everett Millais. The artist was struck by Effie's beauty and asked if she would model for him. Ruskin gave his permission, although he may have regretted it later. In 1853 the three of them went to Scotland on a painting trip. Millais did his famous portrait of Ruskin standing in front of a rushing mountain burn, and began to make quiet love to Effie behind his back. Whether they consummated their love at the time is not recorded but Millais's declarations of love gave Effie the courage to finally confront the unsatisfactory situation of her marriage to Ruskin; for a start, Effie wanted children.

At the end of that year Effie told her parents about the platonic nature of her marriage and with their help filed a case for annulment. Ruskin didn't deny the charges and he didn't try to prevent Effie from leaving. The case was a public curiosity. In 1855 Effie was free to marry Millais, which she did. The marriage was a good one and the couple had eight children. There was a downside, however, in that Effie could not be seen at social events that involved the queen. As Queen Victoria did not regard Effie's annulment of her marriage as

Effie Ruskin

legitimate, she refused to invite her to royal social functions. Some of the aristocracy followed suit and refused to entertain Effie, although they would accept her husband, John Everett Millais. Towards the very end of Millais's life the queen was persuaded by one of her daughters to make an exception to the harsh rule so that Effie could attend an event with him. Effie didn't survive her husband for very long, she died about sixteen months afterwards in 1897.

Ruskin didn't marry again, although when he was in his mid-40s he did propose to a girl of 16. Rose La Touche was 9 when she and Ruskin began a deep and curious friendship. They constantly wrote to each other, she was Rosie Posie and he was Sir Crumpet. The correspondence was encouraged by the child's mother who could see nothing harmful in it. When Rosie turned 16 Ruskin asked her parents if he could marry her. Rosie was as keen as he was. The parents couldn't see any great objection, the age gap was wide but not unheard of and Ruskin would provide a comfortable life for their daughter. Everything was set to go ahead, until Effie Millais heard about it. She felt it her duty, after her own shabby treatment in being Mrs John Ruskin, to warn the parents of the true nature of the prospective groom. Rosie's parents were suitably startled, enough to call it all off and to put a stop to any correspondence between the two. Ruskin was broken-hearted and Rosie fell ill. Although Effie's interference was made from the best of motives, in this odd case perhaps it was the wrong thing to have done. Rosie never recovered and died insane at the age of 26.

BURNE-JONES IN SEARCH OF LOVE

Edward Burne-Jones was a late arrival on the Pre-Raphaelite scene; indeed he is often called the last Pre-Raphaelite. He was tall and thin with light-coloured hair and pale skin. In later years he grew a moustache and beard, which gave him a very distinguished air. In his work he was always looking for perfect beauty and for this he needed suitable models. Burne-Jones lived for his art and could find it difficult to separate reality from artistic inspiration.

In 1856 Burne-Jones became engaged to bonny lass Georgiana Macdonald; she was only 15 and he 22. Georgiana came from a strict Methodist background, and until her fiancé could afford to keep her there was no possibility they would break their celibacy. It wasn't until 1860 that they married. For the next fifteen years or so it was a good, loving marriage seeing the birth of healthy children.

Then in the mid-1860s Edward Burne-Jones, who had been such a faithful husband, began to find his interest straying. He and his family moved into bigger premises that would allow him an extensive studio complex that would have a special, inner sanctum, private from all the comings and goings of family life. Children were noisy, although he adored them; his wife was capable, kind and loving but she had lost her youthful beauty and, while still very good-looking, had taken on a determination as the head of a successful household. Also, sexual relations between husband and wife had stalled, perhaps because they did not want to have any more children (although this is speculation).

Burne-Jones needed stimulation. He needed beauty, romance and personal attention. He needed a new muse. And he found it just before the family moved into their new house. Maria Zambaco was tall, dark haired with large brown eyes. She was in many ways not dissimilar to Jane Morris. Maria was to be a grand passion that would drain the artist emotionally and physically.

Born Maria Terpsithec Cassaretti in 1843, Maria came from a wealthy and influential family with a Greek heritage. Her mother was a famous socialite, Euphrosyne Cassaretti, though often called the duchess. As a child Maria, aged 4, was painted in exotic Turkish costume by the painter G.F. Watts. As she grew up she enjoyed painting and drawing and had thought she might make a career out of it, not that she needed to earn a living as she inherited a large fortune on her father's death when she was still in her teens.

In 1861, against her family's wishes, Maria married a Greek doctor, Demetrius Alexander Zambaco, and went to live with him in Paris.

Maria Zambaco

Zambaco would go on to become an expert in the dermatological effects of syphilis. The marriage lasted hardly five years and Maria was back in London living with her high-society mother. Although Zambaco refused to give her a divorce Maria came home with her fortune intact and the return of her dowry. What made the marriage fail is unknown, although it has been suggested by Maria's family that the good doctor was in fact interested in child pornography. They had two children, Frank and Maria Euphrosyne. Frank had suffered some kind of brain damage at birth or in early childhood.

Maria was wealthy and single (although not free to marry again), she could take up art again but she would need a good teacher. One of the delights of her pre-marriage life was to mingle with the leading lights of the artistic community and Maria was more than happy to return to it. Relatives of her mother had bought a large house and it was here that Burne-Jones was invited, along with many of his friends and colleagues. Maria's mother took great care to introduce the artist to her daughter. In fact she probably did more than was necessary to bring them as close together as possible.

A double portrait of Maria and her best friend Marie Spartali was commissioned by the duchess. Burne-Jones was flattered and more than happy to paint two lovely women, and Maria was more than lovely, she was a goddess. Burne-Jones decided to depict the two friends as Cupid and Psyche. His initial painting was not what he had hoped and he didn't feel he could accept payment for it. It would take months of sketches and drawings before he could present the family with a finished work that he was satisfied with. This may have been an excuse to extend his contact with the woman who was rapidly turning into his latest muse and love interest.

Maria became Burne-Jones's model and pupil and therefore was able to come and go to his private studio without arousing suspicion. Georgiana may have suspected something but chose to keep it to herself if she did. Her husband was always a soft touch for a beautiful woman in distress, and in Maria he found both. Maria was estranged from her brilliant young husband for some unspecified reason, but it must have been serious if it meant she had come back to live with her mother. It is hard for an outsider in another century to look too sadly on Maria's position; she did have wealth and comfort, children and a loving family. Georgiana also had many of these things; though wealth was not one of them, she was comfortably off.

Maria's wealth allowed her a support team who could look after children and household duties; thus she was able to take up her art practice again. Georgiana, on the other hand, although certainly not poor, could not afford such a luxury and had given up all thought of her own artistic dreams when she married. Burne-Jones, wrapped up in his gorgeous new model who was beautiful and clever, could not help feeling tied down by his older and home-obsessed wife. However, it was Georgiana who would stick by him through thick and thin, nurse him when he was ill and keep his finances in check. Without that steady person in the background he, like many other artists and creators, would not have functioned at all. What is more, when she did find an incriminating letter in the pocket of her husband's jacket, Georgiana did not confront him with it but remained as passive as ever.

Maria returned Burne-Jones's passion, even though he was getting on for 40 and she was only in her mid-20s. He drew caricatures of himself as a gawky scarecrow of a fellow, constantly wondering what she saw in him. While the affair was at its height Burne-Jones's work flourished. His output was both prolific and of high quality, but it was not sustainable and nor was the pressure of guilt at betraying his wife.

Finally Burne-Jones tried to break off the affair. Ruskin has left documentation of his friend's attempts and also how they failed. Burne-Jones wanted both his beautiful, rich, fascinating mistress and his loyal, efficient wife, mother of his beloved children. Maria had hatched a plan in which the two of them would run off to a Greek island and live there happily ever after. Burne-Jones, initially excited at the prospect of leaving his ordinary life behind, was tempted for a fleeting moment, before reality brought him to his senses. He could not do that to his family, nor his friends, patrons or himself. It was a fantasy and he knew it; Maria did not.

In 1869 Maria ordered her lover to walk with her in Lord Holland's Lane, where she told him that she was taking enough laudanum to kill herself. They walked, talked, argued, pleaded and tried to reason with each other. By the time they had reached the bridge over Regent's Canal, Maria was in such a state that she tried to throw herself into the water. Burne-Jones grappled with her and they rolled around on the ground. Two policemen turned up, separated the pair, restraining Burne-Jones while trying to get to the bottom of the matter. Luckily Maria's cousin and former lover, probably jealous for her attention, turned up and took charge of Maria, helping her to walk away. It seemed he had known something was up and deliberately followed the pair.

Burne-Jones arrived home in a dreadful state, his nerves were shot to pieces and he was shivering with shock and cold. Georgiana put him straight to bed, no questions asked. William Morris came to the rescue claiming that Burne-Jones could do well to have a little trip to Rome, an artists' inspirational journey. It would get his friend away from the dramatic Maria and give him time to recover. They got as far as Dover and had to go back as Burne-Jones was too ill to travel. For some days after his return home Georgiana pretended he was still away, believing his shattered mind and body needed quiet rest. She even lied to friends about his whereabouts so that nothing would intrude on the healing process.

While his health did revive somewhat he was left in a delicate state. Also, Warrington Taylor, the manager of Morris, Marshall, Faulkner and Co., told both Burne-Jones and Rossetti that their romantic affairs would ruin the firm's reputation if they continued. Burne-Jones, suitably chastened, was filled with guilt. He had been unfaithful to his wife, ruined the life of his beautiful mistress and was possibly damaging his business partners.

Still, none of this stopped Burne-Jones's affair with Maria from continuing, albeit at a less tumultuous level. They saw each other regularly, went out together, stayed in together and fought with each other. Until 1872, that is, when Maria suddenly went to Paris. There is conjecture that she had lined up a new lover in France and as her previous one was not going to sacrifice everything for her she could now afford to toss him aside. Even though things settled down a bit after she left, a correspondence continued between them for years afterwards, and in 1874, during a trip by Burne-Jones to Italy, there is evidence that they met up again and continued where they had left off two years before.

In 1875 a new muse entered Burne-Jones's world. Frances Grahame, the daughter of one of his friends, had grown into a lovely young woman. She was not 20 and Burne-Jones was 40. Although he sent her letters full of his undying love, his grand passion and his need for her, Frances, although flattered and kind was not interested in starting an affair with him. Over the next few years Burne-Jones would continue to press his suit but to no avail. Frances, having married John Horner and started a family, always remained kind and loving to Burne-Jones but was never able to reciprocate the type of love he wanted. Perhaps he would not have known what to do with it if she had. As we have seen, when he had succumbed to the beautiful Maria he had become immensely unsettled and unhappy.

While renewing his pursuit of Frances, Burne-Jones was also declaring his love for another woman, a friend of Frances's, Helen Gaskell. She was 39 to his 58. Helen was another woman in distress, very unhappily married to a man who may well have beaten her. Their meetings had to be kept secret, although it doesn't seem as though the affair had a sexual element to it.

These last two attempts at romantic unions with beautiful women, whom Burne-Jones liked to paint, came to nothing. Before his death he asked all the recipients of his love letters to destroy them as he did not want anything to remain to incriminate him and bring his widow embarrassment. However, most of them did not. Georgiana wrote a biography of her husband but was careful to gloss over areas that were painful to her and to his memory.

Burne-Jones and Georgiana were married for thirty-six years. In all that time she only played the muse for a brief time, but in reality she was the stability behind him that let him indulge in the emotional rides that gave him the inspiration to paint.

Part 6
Mistresses in the Twentieth Century

FLORENCE DUGDALE AND THOMAS HARDY

When Florence Dugdale wrote to Thomas Hardy in 1905 asking if she could meet him, he had already been married to Emma for thirty-five years. They had a convivial marriage although they had stopped sharing a bedroom since 1899. They were companionable but were steadily growing further apart. Hardy had been tempted to have an affair from as early as 1889 when he fell in love with the married Rosamund Tomson, but she was only interested in friendship. Then there was Florence Henniker but she too was only wanting a platonic relationship, flattered by Hardy's attentions but nothing more.

Then Florence Dugdale's letter came out of the blue, telling the writer how much she loved his work and she really wanted to meet him. Although Hardy received fan mail he had never received this kind of request before and he invited her to come to his house, Max Gate. By chance or design Emma was not there. Lunch was very enjoyable and Hardy invited Florence to come again.

Florence Dugdale

Hardy was in need of a muse and he thought he might just have found her in pretty, young and intelligent Florence Dugdale. For her part, Florence enjoyed having someone to admire, or at least she pretended she did. What her motives were it is difficult to tell. She was an aspiring writer and maybe wanted a helping hand in getting work published, or she may have been genuinely a keen fan.

Florence was one of five daughters of the headmaster of a Church of England School at Enfield, north London, and a staunch supporter of the Conservative Party. She became a pupil-teacher at her father's school when she was 15 until it became too much for her and she took a position as a lady's companion in 1906. What she really wanted was to be a writer. One of the things that make Florence's motives for Hardy's friendship questionable is the way she has distorted the truth about certain aspects of how they met and what her true employment was. For a start, she didn't want to publicly admit she was a paid companion, instead she told people she was just visiting friends, staying with them for a while. Then there were some curious anomalies in her tale about meeting Hardy. She never admitted she had written to him as a complete stranger and invited herself to his house. She gave a couple of different accounts for this. One was that she had met the Hardys while out walking with a friend, they got chatting and she was invited back to their house; another version has Florence Henniker introducing her to the Hardys as a couple. The latter story cannot be true because Florence Dugdale did not become acquainted with Florence Henniker until well after she had established her friendship with Hardy.

The old lady to whom Florence had been hired as companion finally had to go into a nursing home. Her husband, Sir Thornley Stoker, had enjoyed having Florence about the place. He had given her a typewriter when he discovered she wanted to be a writer and then on his wife's death gave her a ring. Florence used her typewriter a lot, teaching herself to touch type. Finding out that Florence could type gave Hardy an excuse to see more of her. She would type for him, something that she later used as a step up the ladder by stating she had been his secretary. Hardy also got her to undertake research for his work. In return he sent letters of introduction to newspapers and publishers recommending her work and Florence began to carve out a career for herself as a writer.

Hardy fell in love with Florence; he took her on holidays, wrote her letters and praised her writing (when in fact, according to opinion, it was really quite ordinary). One thing he did not intend, though, was to leave his wife Emma. It was years before Emma and Florence met, and their eventual meeting had nothing to do with Hardy. Emma was to give a talk at the Lyceum Club of which Florence was a member. On hearing of this Florence asked Hardy if she should introduce herself. Hardy was very encouraging.

Instead of being a rival for her husband's affection, Emma found Florence as admiring of her as she was of Hardy. Florence was good at flattery. She liked to make people feel good, although she had her own reasons for doing so, usually to do with her ambition.

What transpired was another triangle: Hardy, Emma and Florence. Both Emma and Thomas Hardy loved Florence, both wanted her attention and sometimes the result was disastrous, such as the Christmas of 1910 when Florence spent it with the Hardys at Max Gate. Hardy told Emma he wanted to take Florence to meet his family. Emma was very angry and told him that they were sure to try their hardest to make Florence hate her. Emma stormed out of the room and Florence swore to herself she would never spend a Christmas with the pair again.

Then at the end of November 1912 Emma died suddenly after complaining of feeling unwell. She had gone to bed one evening, agreed to see the doctor but refused to let him actually examine her. She died the following morning from heart failure.

Hardy was not thought to be able to manage on his own. Although he had several domestic staff he needed a housekeeper. There were two contenders for the position: Florence, of course, and Emma's niece Lilian. Katie, Hardy's sister, had stepped in for the interim. Lilian probably wanted to escape living with her mother and saw her uncle's situation as perfect; she'd be head of the household, a woman with influence and authority, she'd also be able to entertain Hardy's interesting guests, all in a highly respectable situation. However, Katie and Florence couldn't stand Lilian; she was domineering and snobbish, especially to Florence. Lilian was out to make trouble; not only did she want the position for herself but she wanted to know what Florence had to do with her uncle, she spread rumours about Florence that began to cause problems for Hardy.

Emma's death had been a shock to Hardy. He had probably taken her for granted then when she suddenly wasn't there any more he began a period of profound reminiscing. These thoughts and memories were set down as a series of poems, which became some of his greatest work. To escape into the past was a glorious way of avoiding his present problems, which involved who was going to do what at Max Gate. Hardy wanted to please everyone and himself; he wanted to avoid scandal but did not want to lose Florence, who was still very much the object of his passion. Yet at the same time all he wanted to do was think about his life with Emma. Eventually he asked Florence to marry him, thinking that by making her mistress of the house all problems would be sorted. Yet it wasn't going to work that easily. Lilian had been poisoning the staff against Florence and if she continued in the house there would always be an undermining of Florence's authority.

In the end it was Florence who sorted out the mess: either Lilian went or she did, she would not marry him. Hardy packed poor Lilian off home, although he did it very kindly and kept in touch with her for the rest of his life.

On 10 February 1914, Thomas Hardy and Florence Dugdale came together at last. If it was Florence's fairy tale come true then she didn't seem to enjoy it that much. She was constantly feeling jealous over Hardy's memories and poems about Emma. The four years after Emma's death were some of his most productive, especially for writing poetry. Florence found her husband's absorption in his work to be a source of contention in their relationship. It is a wonder though, that having wanted to be a writer herself, she did not understand Hardy's need to work. Often it is exactly that which attracts someone to a person that in the end pushes them away. Florence stuck by Hardy, worked as his secretary and sounding board. She seemed happy to work on anything that didn't involve Emma.

In the last few weeks of Hardy's life Florence stayed as close to him as she could, reading to him, chatting and attending to his needs. Yet it seems she may not have been there for his last words and final breath, which were given to Florence's sister Eva when Hardy called her name saying, 'What is this?'

Hardy left an estate worth £100,000 (around £212,000 in today's money). It was broken up into bequests to charities and various relatives (the bulk going to his brother and sister). Florence was left the house, Max Gate, granted income from all Hardy's royalties and a small annuity of £600. If she were to remarry this sum would halve. This was not Hardy being mean to his second wife, it was a standard clause to protect widows from being tricked into marriage by men just after their money.

What did surprise Hardy's friend Sydney Cockerill was the fact that Florence had entered into an engagement with the writer J.M. Barrie only half a year after her husband's death. The marriage never took place, Barrie getting cold feet and breaking off the engagement. Florence was both shocked and upset by his actions but they did remain friends. Perhaps in marrying Florence, Barrie had hoped to hold on to some last shred of his friend Hardy, but as time moved on he realised it would not work. When Barrie died in 1937 Florence was very sad. Yet she had another problem of her own to face, she had been diagnosed with bowel cancer and did not live much longer after Barrie's death.

REBECCA WEST AND H.G. WELLS

Rebecca West is known in her own right as a writer and intellectual. She was also, for a time, the second main woman in the life of H.G. Wells; she was for all her ideas of freedom for women, his mistress. Free love may have been the motto that both writers subscribed to, but when you look at the fact that Rebecca lived hidden away in an insignificant house, pretending not to be the mother of her son Anthony, one can't help thinking there are echoes of times gone by when illegitimate births were seen as indiscretions to be concealed.

Rebecca West was born Cicely Isabel Fairfield but took up the pen name of Rebecca West after seeing a production of the Ibsen play *Rosmersholm*, which has a character of that name in it. Rebecca was writing for a radical women's paper called *New Free Woman* but, despite the free thinking of the women in her own family, she thought that it was a good idea to keep her real identity under wraps, so as not to cause embarrassment.

Wells met Rebecca after she had written a lengthy review of one his latest books, the novel *Marriage*. In the article she calls Wells 'the old maid among novelists' and accused him of writing about sex with a mind that had been too long obsessed with science fiction. When Wells read the review he was intrigued and invited the little-known female writer to lunch, probably hoping that an animated debate would ensue. That first visit lasted well into the afternoon.

Wells's first wife was his cousin, the beautiful and animated Isabel Mary. He met her in 1886 but they didn't marry until 1891. Wells was to write about this first serious relationship in his autobiography, saying that he'd been made to wait to marry Isabel and that he was made to marry her in a church and that, actually, he didn't believe in the institution of marriage anyway. Almost immediately things went wrong and in 1892 Wells met Amy Catherine Robbins.

Two years later, after the divorce with Isabel, Wells married Amy whom he renamed Jane. Jane was to become the mainstay of his life; she knew about all his affairs, stating that she realised he needed extended times to be alone or to do his own thing. The first time Wells showed any sign of needing his own space was after the birth of their first child, a boy, George Philip in 1901. Wells just disappeared.

Jane, with what became her trademark elastic attitude to her husband's self-centred needs, told him that she would give him all the time and space he needed whenever he wanted it. This was probably how she kept him married to her. Wells described Jane as being delicate and ethereal, and at her funeral gave an elegy that was described by some as a total myth. One family friend said that Jane had been one of the strongest women they'd ever known. Wells's words of farewell to his dead wife make one wonder if his wife was perhaps the greatest of his muses and his mistresses were just for fun.

H.G. Wells

West met Wells in 1912 and after their initial meeting an affair soon began. Rebecca has been likened to Ann Veronica, the heroine of one of Wells's novels, calling on her married lover to make love to her. Whether this is true or not, the idea that the young writer was influenced by the older writer's work and using it as a catalyst to bring them together makes the idea of mistress as muse particularly interesting: West may have become Wells's muse but it certainly worked the other way too. Although the affair started passionately enough and involved two advocates of free love, it was Wells who first broke it off.

Wells was already involved with a woman he termed his mistress, Elizabeth Von Arnim, another writer. Perhaps Elizabeth was not as accommodating about sharing her lover as Jane was about sharing her husband, but the outcome was that Wells fled overseas. Before he left he told Rebecca that they would have to break off all communication between them, he couldn't even stay her friend. Unable to understand or accept the huge wrench, Rebecca was on the point of suicide.

The young woman's sensible mother took her daughter off to the Continent for an extended trip through France and Spain. Rebecca wrote and then published accounts of her travels and Wells, on reading these, initiated a reunion between them, telling her that her writing was 'gorgeous' and that he wanted them to be friends again. At this point in the history of the love affair, the modern reader begins to have doubts as to their sincerity in anything. Whilst both Wells and West were supporters of feminism, West reacted like the heroine of some soppy romance and Wells was behaving like a typical male chauvinist. Still, theory doesn't always play out in practice. What Wells perhaps didn't tell Rebecca was that his affair with Von Arnim (who Wells refers to as 'little e') was over and he was free to take another lover – or he needed consolation.

The outcome was that by 1914 Rebecca West was pregnant with Wells's child. Jane was told straightaway. She had already known about the existence of another illegitimate child by Amber Reeves (also a writer). Amber was born in New Zealand but went to England with her parents to finish school and attend university. She and her parents were members of the Fabian Society. After Amber had given

Rebecca West

a student paper at the Philosophical Society, where she met Wells, it is said the couple went to Paris for a weekend alone. It soon became public knowledge that Amber and Wells were lovers. Wells was all for hiding the relationship but Amber couldn't understand why. It wasn't difficult for the people around them to discover the affair. One friend of the Wellses stated that the scandal was in the fact that the affair wasn't kept hidden.

In 1909 Amber Reeves was pregnant. She and Wells removed to France to get away from all the gossip. The two of them were hopeless at living together, neither wanted the responsibility of housework or cooking. This may well explain part of the reason that Wells was so grateful to his wife Jane, as she buffered him from mundane reality. Amber couldn't cope at all and was packed off back to England by Wells while he remained overseas to write. When he too returned home, he and Jane took Amber into their house to live with them.

Before Wells's baby was born in December 1909 Amber married a lawyer, George Rivers Blanco White. In her own writing she says that it was not a marriage of her choice but one made between White and Wells. She concedes it was one of the best things to have ever happened to her. The daughter, Anna-Jane, born on the last day of the year, was under the impression her father was White; when she turned 18 she was told the truth.

Six years later Wells's latest mistress, Rebecca West, was about to give birth in a rather unattractive semi-detached house in an out of the way place: Hunstanton in Norfolk. She and Wells began an elaborate charade of being husband and wife. Wells became Mr West, a movie director, although sometimes he said he was a journalist. The child, Anthony, was brought up to call his father 'Wellsie' and his mother 'Auntie Panther'. This was something that Anthony, as an adult, found very hard to forgive his mother for.

Wells and West kept their relationship going all through the war years. Jane and Rebecca were expected to be courteous to each other. Jane had grown used to this and saw it as an aspect of her wifely duties to her genius husband. Rebecca also played her part towards Jane with politeness. However, scratch the surface of these two women and what they really felt for each other was quite a different matter. Jane would go through all the letters Wells received, whether they were business or private – this was also part of her duty. With the love letters Jane would annotate them at their points of hypocrisy in regards to herself. Rebecca in turn would privately comment that Jane was a dominating witch. Wells, whatever his extraordinary charm was that made these otherwise independent and intelligent women fall over themselves for him, was unconcerned at the reality behind the façade; as long as he was happy then that was all that mattered. Apparently, when he took Rebecca and baby Anthony for a ride in his car, he later complained to Rebecca that all the attention focused on the baby and that it really made him question his love for her.

Jane, on the other hand, was his ideal: organised, domesticated and totally devoted to making his life comfortable. Why did someone like Rebecca West want the company of such a man? Love is blind the old maxim goes and perhaps it is true. The relationship between the writers was already beginning to show signs of strain. Rebecca had to resort to journalism to help pay the bills, while she longed to have the leisure to write what she considered serious work. Wells would have kept her financially, although maybe not in luxury, but Rebecca was adamant to stay independent. Anthony was a nuisance to her writing and at the age of 4, or even before that, he was sent to a Montessori boarding school. Anthony later wrote very bitterly about his childhood experiences and could not see how getting rid of him so early meant that she had ever loved him.

Rebecca began to tire of having to share her lover with his wife and the other demands on his time. On his side, Wells got insanely jealous at any suggestion that Rebecca might be seeing another man. Rebecca would quarrel with her domestic employees and this made the household constantly unsettled. Wells was so used to the domestic quiet and smooth running of the house he shared with Jane that he kept bringing up the comparison in front of Rebecca. At one point he had Jane send Rebecca a housekeeper, but the woman was so awful that Rebecca told her to leave. Anthony, sticking up for his mother instead of maligning her, suggests that the offer of help from Jane to Rebecca was in fact a veiled insult.

In 1922 Rebecca and Wells met in Gibraltar to begin a holiday in Spain. The reunion was highly anticipated by Rebecca at least and she wrote of how she couldn't wait to see him. The holiday was a disaster. Wells was ill, or thought he was. His complaints and irritability with everything around him, including his nursemaid, infuriated Rebecca. When she herself had been ill in the past Wells had never had any sympathy or patience with her. Then, to Rebecca's absolute horror and disgust, Wells ordered her to get his coat from their room before they went out for a walk. It was not a request but a command and it was made in a hotel foyer full of people. Rebecca made an equally public negation to his demand.

What both of them wanted was a caring wife-like figure. Wells already had this in Jane; unfortunately he also wanted sexual excitement and constant stimulation from other sources. Rebecca probably wanted someone to coset her and adore her while letting her follow her career. In other words, the two writers were very similar and therefore totally wrong for each other in any kind of domestic relationship.

Apparently Rebecca, after her mother's death in 1921, began referring to Wells as her husband when she wrote to him. Over the next seven or eight years the relationship between Wells and West was as tempestuous as ever. They would fight and make up repeatedly. When Jane died of cancer in 1927 Rebecca was worried that she would have to become a Jane substitute and be stifled under the domesticity of looking after a literary genius instead of being one.

Finally the affair ended when Rebecca married Henry Andrews, a respectable banker. This man was to provide the stability and care that she craved for herself. She may have desired the excitement of Wells but when it came to reality, Rebecca West needed financial and emotional support. She settled into middle-class respectability very well and at times bemoaned the fact that she had wasted so much time and energy on loving Wells. The two remained friends until Wells's death in 1946. Even though Rebecca West had been happily married for nearly twenty years by the time Wells died, she mourned his loss deeply.

THE WOMEN OF RADCLYFFE HALL

Radclyffe Hall

Marguerite Radclyffe-Hall was born on 12 August 1880 of very wealthy, landowning stock. In 1907 she met the woman who would be her first great passion, Mabel Batten, twenty-three years her senior and already a grandmother. Mabel was a very gifted amateur singer and was herself married to an older man. Mabel had had affairs on and off throughout her marriage and if her husband minded he never let it show.

Marguerite, who took the name Radclyffe as a first name, began a steamy affair with Mabel. Again, Mabel's husband seemed perfectly happy for his wife to amuse herself in this way. On his death Mabel and Radclyffe set up house together. Mabel decided to call her lover John and that was the name that stuck ever afterwards.

Before life with Mabel, John had harboured ambitions to be a writer but had never committed to actually doing it. Under Mabel's influence and direction, she began to write seriously. It was Mabel who introduced her partner to William Heinemann of the publishing house and on his advice John began writing her first novel. Mabel was always the womanly half of the couple while John had always enjoyed dressing up like a boy and was happy to continue that way. Mabel tended to mother John; after all, she had years of experience and John's own mother had never been very interested in her daughter.

In 1915 an afternoon tea party was held by Lady Clarendon. John and Mabel were invited as was a much younger cousin of Mabel's. Her name at birth was Margot Elena Gertrude Taylor, although she preferred Una. Her married name was Troubridge and her title was Lady. Una had a young daughter, Andrea. Admiral Troubridge had three children from his first marriage, had obviously been a bit of a womaniser and gave Una syphilis; it was not a happy union.

At the time of that fateful tea party Mabel and John had been together for eight years. John was prone to falling in love on the spot and had a few flings here and there, but mostly she was dedicated to a life with Mabel, whom she would never leave. Una was introduced to John and it was love at first sight. Mabel was content to let the passion run its usual course and abate. However, this time it didn't. John and Una saw more and more of each other, sometimes in Mabel's company but more often than not alone.

By the end of the year the three were on holiday together in Cornwall. Two's company but three's a crowd proved true in this

Mabel Batten

case. Mabel complained of tiredness and stayed most of the time in her room reading while the two younger women rambled about by themselves. For Mabel, the holiday was a disaster and she told John that although she didn't mind her having a younger lover, she did not like being part of a threesome. John was free to see Una but not in Mabel's company and not all the time. John retorted that Mabel was being overly possessive and jealous, reminding Mabel that she didn't own her.

After a particularly bad quarrel over dinner one night Mabel took a funny turn. At first John thought it was a dramatic tantrum but it soon became apparent that something serious was wrong. Mabel felt terribly cold, had pins and needles in her legs and was getting sharp pains through her chest. She collapsed and was carted off to hospital. Mabel Batten had suffered a cerebral haemorrhage. She slipped in and out of consciousness over the next ten days. She tried to communicate with John but was not able to form words. John was with her when she died.

Filled with remorse and plagued by guilt John refused to see Una. She blamed herself for Mabel's death, thinking it was the row that had caused it. Una was upset for her own sake, fearing that her new-found love was over before it had begun. After some time they reconciled and Una agreed to accompany John to a spiritual medium to see if they could make contact with Mabel and get advice from her. They were lucky and Mabel's spirit was able to forgive John and to hand over her welfare to Una.

Grieving for Mabel and contacting her spirit on a regular basis (sometimes up to five times a week) brought John and Una together. Una had never felt anything for Mabel except perhaps resentment but she went along with the game to humour John, whom she was in love with more and more. They made shrines to Mabel in the houses they lived in and put together a long paper to present to the Society for Psychical Research, based on their observations during all the séances they had had for Mabel.

John had become enthralled with the spirit world and was keen to become a member of the council of the Society for Psychical Research. The contents of the paper that she and Una had given had let slip the trio's sexuality. John Lane Fox-Pitt, an established

Una Troubridge

member of the society, was scandalised that someone of that ilk could be on the council and claimed that the other John was guilty of gross immorality. Fox-Pitt went to Una's husband to see if he would be backed up if he were to bring a charge against the pair. Admiral Troubridge did feel his wife was losing her grip on reality and that the affair between the two women was disgusting. The charge was made formal and a trial was held. It caused a sensation; the courtroom was packed with spectators anticipating a good show with lots of juicy sex talk.

The pair of lovers came dressed in fashionable ladies' clothes, wearing hats, gloves and all. John had decided, or Una had persuaded her, that appearance would make a huge difference to the outcome of the trial – and they were the stars of the show. But there wasn't going to be a show after all. Una's husband in a fit of nerves withdrew his evidence, which left Fox-Pitt standing against the women on his own. In a fast bit of back-pedalling, he too withdrew the accusation and tried to say that he had never made them in the first place. John was awarded £500 damages. How the business came to trial is confusing, as in 1920 lesbianism wasn't a crime quite simply because it didn't exist (according to the law). Triumphant, John and Una went back to a quiet life.

Over the next five years the couple settled down into a marriage-type arrangement. The passion of their early love was no longer there but the comfortable domesticity was. John concentrated on writing while Una hovered in the background to help her do it. In 1928 John's best known work *The Well of Loneliness*, a frank examination of the problems confronting lesbian love, was published by Jonathan Cape. It did not at first cause a scandal. In fact some of the reviews suggested it was rather boring, claiming that was the worst thing about it. And if that had been all that was said about it then the book probably would have disappeared into obscurity.

The *Sunday Express* unexpectedly ran an editorial on it, claiming it was poisonous filth and damaging to public morality. In defence of *The Well of Loneliness* the publishers tried to pull together some big literary names but no one really wanted to be involved. It was not the subject matter so much as the book was not deemed worthy of all the fuss. Virginia Woolf admitted that it put her to sleep, it was so tediously written. Still, fifty-seven writers and critics were ready to testify in the book's defence but the judge told them that their evidence would not be needed. He had already made up his mind and the book was banned.

It was already in the process of being printed in Paris and it soon hit the bookshops there with a bang. It became an instant bestseller thanks to the judge's decision. Copies were smuggled into England and John became a writing sensation and women's hero. It was not actually what she had wanted. John had been serious in trying to express the trouble and pain felt by someone in her position. In many ways she seems to have been a man trapped in a female body, and a conservative one at that. She could not understand the fuss made against the book nor of that made for it – and she didn't like either.

It was five or six years later that Evguenia entered the lives of John and Una, in much the same way as Una had into John and Mabel's. It wasn't as a guest that the Russian woman became known to them but as a nurse to Una when she got food poisoning. John was smitten in exactly the manner that she had been with Una. Passion, lust and infatuation.

The couple of weeks spent nursing Una gave time for John to observe and discover her feelings for Evguenia. The couple went on a date after Una was convalescing and Evguenia asked John to kiss her. From there the affair escalated quickly. John sent Evguenia numerous little gifts. Then she began to pay for her rent and living expenses. With the financial support came John's desire to dominate her new lover. Evguenia was not allowed to work, she was not allowed to do this or that, or to see whomever she wanted. If John was holding the purse strings then Evguenia had to comply with her wishes. One solution would have been to refuse to accept the money, although Evguenia confessed it made life a lot easier not having to earn for oneself. When Evguenia did not do what John requested or ordered John would punish her in some way as if she were a child (although such punishments were childish in themselves, as if the two women were playing at being father and daughter).

Manipulation worked both ways and Evguenia was just as clever at keeping John on tenterhooks. She would tell John she was unsure of her true sexual nature, that she did quite admire men so perhaps she wasn't a real lesbian. She would also suggest that there were other attractive women options around.

Una was unhappy during all of this. John would want to agonise to her over Evguenia but Una didn't want to know, she was jealous and hurt, just as Mabel had been all those years before when John had felt the same way about Una.

The three went on holiday, just as John and Una had with Mabel. Una tended to be left out, just as her predecessor had been. However, Evguenia was not particularly happy either. She tired of John's games and her possessiveness, and she didn't know if she really did want to continue in a lesbian affair, and certainly not in a jealous threesome.

In amongst the violent tantrums that John displayed in front of Evguenia when she didn't get her own way, and when she was not moaning and groaning over not seeing her, John would tell Una how much she still loved and needed her, the mainstay of their relationship, in the way she had reassured Mabel.

By 1937 and with war looming in Europe, Evguenia became more interested in world affairs. John could not understand that there could be something more consuming than herself. She had sponsored Evguenia so she could live in England as the war broke. Evguenia took a typing course, against John's wishes, and got a job with the Foreign Office. The position was important and interesting and John resented it because it meant that Evguenia was living independently of her – and if that happened then John might be in danger of losing her, which she was. Evguenia was truly sick of the situation; she had borne it for nine years already and it was time to stop.

Evguenia kept in touch with John and would chide Una for not watching John's alcohol consumption. Una still hated Evguenia, even if she was right about John's health. She saw the woman as nothing but an intrusion on what had been a blissful domestic union. When John had an operation on her eyes and was left unable to read or write for a few weeks, Una took care of all correspondence, including letters to Evguenia. Una at last had some control herself and made sure that much of what John dictated was heavily edited.

In 1943 John's health had deteriorated even more and she was finally diagnosed with bowel cancer. It was the ever faithful Una who nursed her, although Evguenia would visit when she could. Una didn't like her coming and tried to prevent her from touching John if she could. On her deathbed John, who had once in a fit of deep love told Evguenia she'd leave her a large sum of money when she died, revoked that wish and left her whole estate and fortune to Una on the condition that she make an allowance for Evguenia.

Una mourned her partner deeply and even had her suits cut to size so that she could wear them. She styled herself on John for many years afterwards. Finally Una found a new object to fawn over and serve in the way she had John. This time it was an Italian opera singer and he was male.

Evguenia ended up marrying a Russian émigré with whom she lived in poverty. She called on Una's charity and compassion when she was also diagnosed with cancer but Una, still hurting from John's betrayal, refused. Evguenia had her meagre allowance and that was all she was going to get from Una.

Una died in 1963.

Part 7
Mistresses of Men of the Common Class

The last section of this book was extremely difficult to write. I needed to find stories of ordinary men with ordinary mistresses who led ordinary lives; not princes, or dukes or poets but businessmen, shop-keepers, teachers or taxi drivers. Their histories are not recorded in the same way or to the same extent because they are not famous. The scandals caused by their sexual indiscretions are not the stuff that newspapers are made on, unless they involve perversion or murder or something sensational. Where does one turn to for stories about these men and women?

Thank goodness for the Internet and social networking media! A single call out across the world for help and often it is given. In choosing to rely on word of mouth accounts from living people about their friends and relatives the writer has to be very careful. First, permission has to be sought from the narrator and the family, where possible. Second, names and other identifying information need to be sorted out as to whether real names or substitute ones are given. Third, there is no guarantee that the stories or the details of the stories are true unless there is documentation.

In my own family history there is mention of a remittance man on my mother's side. The mother of the boy was paid to leave England for Australia with her illegitimate son and never to return or try to reconnect with the child's father. No news stories were to appear concerning the child's parentage and a fair sum would be given for them to start a new life on the other side of the world. The family story is that it was the bastard son of Albert Edward, Prince of Wales, later to be Edward VII. And the mother was probably some poor maid who took the roving eye of a prince and got put in the family way. But we don't know. The mother of the child did as she was paid to do and kept her previous history a secret.

On telling my first cousin this story we amazed each other in discovering that she also had a similar tale only with someone from her father's side, and to whom I am no blood relation, perhaps. Now, maybe the stories were made up to help gloss over the truth that girls got pregnant when they shouldn't and by someone they shouldn't (possibly just the boy up the road) and they invent a fairy tale myth to help take the sting out of the truth. Or perhaps there are many similar tales told all over Australia because Edward VII, as king and prince, had a notorious appetite for pretty women.

The first tale I am going to relate was told to me by an acquaintance of mine. It is not something from her own family but her husband's family and she has asked me to cover up the identities of those concerned, although she admitted that names hadn't been given when she heard the story.

MISTRESS FOR A FORTNIGHT

At the beginning of the Great Depression there was huge unemployment, in Australia just as in Britain or the US. Men had to travel across the country looking for work or they were put on to work programmes in return for a pension. Among the unemployed there were many men who had fought in the First World War, thus there was bitterness and desperation.

The family of the woman concerned in this account lived in and around a large country town, west of the Blue Mountains in New South Wales (which in turn are immediately west of Sydney). It was a big Catholic family with numerous cousins and aunts, uncles and extras (sometimes in these families babies born to girls before they get married are absorbed into the general chaos of the family and no one is ever sure who the baby belongs to).

One of the teenage daughters of the family, called Jane (not her real name), went to work at a neighbour's dairy farm. She didn't get paid much but it all helped. She would have had to get up early in time for the first milking. They had milking machines but the cows had to be got into their bales and the machines attached to the udders, then everything had to be cleaned out afterwards. My mother's family had a dairy farm in a different part of the state and she said it was hard getting up so early, especially in winter, when her hands would get frozen.

There were other people employed by the farmer and some of them were itinerant workers. One of these was a young man called Geoff (not his real name). He made himself very amiable to the other workers and people he met in the town. Dances were held regularly at the church hall and, as there weren't many places for young people to go for amusement it was a very popular and well-attended event. Jane would go with two or three of her siblings. Apparently she and Geoff became very friendly and were soon thought to be an item. Days off were spent together; he was introduced to Jane's family – her brothers got on with him, her mum liked to feed him up and he played with the little kids.

Geoff came from Sydney, he said. His father had been killed in the First World War and his mother lived with her mother and father in a cramped semi-detached house in Chippendale. Geoff's grandad wasn't well and his grandmother wasn't too good either, it was a lot for his mum to take care of. She also took in washing and ironing for people.

When Geoff lost his job at the brewery he felt he had to go looking for work out of town. There was nothing for someone like him in the city and he didn't want to be a burden to his mother. He did miss the city though, he admitted. Of course he was full of stories about Sydney. Its delights and entertainments and its dangers, possibly exaggerated to enhance his exoticism. He told them he'd never seen a cow till he got off the train in the country. Another bit of leg pulling probably.

Jane's family wanted to know what he was planning to do when things looked up. Would he stay in the country and get work there or would he go back to Sydney to his old job? Or would he move on somewhere else? The answers were evasive but that may have been because he truly didn't know what the future would hold in the way of job prospects.

Then one day Jane came home from work in tears. Geoff had gone. He'd left. There was no forwarding address, no Sydney address, nothing. Jane was inconsolable. After a few weeks it became apparent as to why she didn't get over it. In a little while Jane went to visit an aunt who lived further away. She'd be staying a while to recover from her broken heart. When she returned, low and behold, somehow another child had appeared in the crowded household. Everyone believed it to be a late baby of Jane's parents, one last one.

Jane did settle down, she did get over the disappearance of Geoff, and maybe even she started thinking that the youngest member of the family was a sibling rather than her own child. After a couple of years Jane got married to a local boy, John (not his real name) and they had two children of their own.

Just before the outbreak of the Second World War Geoff returned; he was his old affable self and full of apologies and regrets. His mother had written to him telling him his grandad had died and she needed him back home. He'd left as quickly as he could, which meant he couldn't say goodbye. And then he'd been offered a job at a printers and he couldn't refuse an opportunity like that. Then his mum had got ill with cancer and he'd had to help nurse her and work too. Things kept preventing him from coming back to see his friends. After a while, he thought, they'd have forgotten about him and he ended up marrying someone from his work.

Jane had thought she was happily settled with her reliable husband and their children. She no longer had to work on the dairy farm and she was well looked after. Whether anyone thought about the baby she'd had, and that he was probably Geoff's son, wasn't mentioned and Geoff didn't seem to have been made aware of him. Geoff stayed in town for a week and then left, making sure to say his farewells this time. And everything went back to normal. Until a month later when Jane suddenly left her husband and kids. She didn't leave a note but she was seen catching a train to the city.

What happened to Jane in Sydney is largely speculation. She had not got over Geoff's disappearance and had followed him back to the city. He had left an address this time, for his workplace, not his home. Jane had taken what money she had, enough for a train trip and a couple of nights in a hotel. She saw Geoff, who had hoped she would follow him, and he paid for her to stay a fortnight in the hotel.

Geoff was married, true, but he was desperately unhappy. His wife wanted him to succeed in business, to climb the social ladder and to keep up their level of living. He told Jane he was sick of it, he'd never really loved his wife and had thought of nothing but finding his Jane again. And she fell for it.

The plan was for Geoff to tell his wife he was leaving her and then he and Jane would find a small flat somewhere, far enough from the abandoned wife so she couldn't make trouble but close enough so he could see his kids. Jane waited every day for his return from work, when she would spend time with Geoff and ask if he'd told his wife about them yet. Each time he gave an excuse for not telling her. It was harder than he thought, he said, he really didn't want to hurt her more than he could help it. Jane needed to be patient.

On the second to last day of the fortnight Geoff came to the hotel late. He was in a bad mood and needed cheering up, he said. They went to dinner and then back to the hotel, and then Geoff announced he had to tell her something. Jane could probably already tell that is wasn't good news for her. Geoff had decided it wasn't possible for him to leave his wife after all. They'd talked hard and long about it and they'd decided to give their marriage another go. Geoff was so sorry, but he needed to think of his family.

Maybe Jane made a scene but if she did it was to no effect. Geoff kissed her and left, telling her not to try to contact him, or his wife would call the police. What a slap in the face. There was no option for Jane except to pack her bag and spend her last amount of money on her train ticket home.

John took her back, no questions asked; the children were thrilled to see mummy after her holiday. And that was the end of the matter.

Jane was pregnant but she never knew if it was her husband's child or her lover's, but this time she made sure it was hers.

THE TWO-FAMILY MAN

The second story is set in England and begins in the 1970s. Again the names will be fictional as none were given in the original version I heard. The man in this story I will call Trevor; he was the headmaster of a primary school and a good upstanding citizen. He was married to Helen and they had four children. As headmaster Trevor often had to stay back at school working late; there was marking to do, reports to be written and there were endless meetings. None of this was out of the ordinary for a man in his position. The kids who went to his school and then on to the local comprehensive were a conscientious lot and all did well enough to go to university.

When Trevor's own children left home he decided to retire. Helen thought that at last they'd have some time together, perhaps travel, move to the seaside. But Trevor was reluctant to move. They did have a couple of holidays abroad but Trevor was always a bit anxious about getting home again. And then he decided to take on some casual teaching work. His pension wasn't really adequate, although Helen didn't see why that should be so, but the money wasn't there so she agreed to let him do more teaching if that's what he really wanted. Trevor continued teaching for several years into his retirement and then he had to stop as he had a stroke. And then he died.

It was at the funeral that the truth came out. Trevor had been leading a double life. He was married to Helen but some years after their marriage he fell in love with a much younger woman and set up house with her. They didn't live that far away from his house with Helen, although the children from his relationship with his mistress didn't go to the same school he taught at. His mistress knew all about the wife but Helen knew nothing about the mistress. Trevor had been so careful, so organised, so businesslike that it seemed impossible for a man like that to have been so devious. He'd even called his children with his mistress the same names as the ones he had with Helen so that he wouldn't get caught out saying the wrong thing and arousing suspicion. The two women were polite to each other but that was all. The children from both sides, however, were intrigued that their father had been so interesting and they all enjoyed having extra siblings.

Acknowledgements

Thank you to my darling daughter Beatriz Alvarez who helped research and edit this book. Also, many thanks to lovely Isabel Atherton of Creative Authors, who gets me the best books. Thanks to Lindsey Smith and the team at The History Press for putting together such a wonderful publication.

Bibliography

Abbot, Elizabeth, *Mistresses, a History of the Other Woman* (Duckworth Overlook: London, 2003)

Blanch, Lesley (ed.), *Harriette Wilson's Memoirs* (Century Publishing: London, 1985)

Bodanis, David, *Passionate Minds* (Little Brown: London, 2006)

Brekke, Tone and Mee, John (eds), *Mary Wollstonecraft: Letters Written During a Short Residence in Sweden, Norway, and Denmark* (Oxford University Press: Oxford, 2009)

Charmley, John, *The Princess and the Politicians* (Viking: London, 2005)

De Beer, E.S. (ed.), *The Diary of John Evelyn* (Everyman's Library: London, 2006)

De Vries, Susanna, *Royal Mistresses* (Pirgos Press: Brisbane, 2012)

Douglas-Fairhurst, Robert, *Becoming Dickens* (The Belknap Press of Harvard University Press: Cambridge, Massachusetts and London, England, 2011)

Foot, Michael, *H.G.: The History of Mr Wells* (Doubleday: Great Britain, 1996)

Foreman, Amanda, *The Duchess* (Harper Perennial: London, 1998)

Fraser, Antonia, *King Charles II* (Weidenfeld & Nicolson: London, 1979)

Fraser, Antonia, *The Weaker Vessel* (Methuen: London, 1984)

Fraser, Antonia, *Love Letters: An Anthology* (Weidenfeld & Nicolson: London, 1976)

Garwood, Christine, *Mid-Victorian Britain* (Shire Publications Ltd: Oxford, 2011)

Griffin, Susan, *The Book of the Courtesans* (Macmillan: London, 2002)

Hahn, Daniel, *Poetic Lives: Shelley* (Hesperus Press Ltd: London, 2009)

Hartley, Jenny (ed.), *The Selected Letters of Charles Dickens* (Oxford University Press: Oxford, 2012)

Hay, Daisy, *Young Romantics* (Farrer, Straus and Giroux: New York, 2010)

Hoppen, K. Theodore, *The Mid-Victorian Generation 1846–1886* (Clarendon Press: Oxford, 1998)

Johnson, Claudia L. (ed.), *The Cambridge Companion to Mary Wollstonecraft* (Cambridge University Press: Cambridge, 2002)

Johnson, Wendell Stacy, *Living in Sin* (Nelson-Hall: Chicago, 1979)

Lutz, Deborah, *Pleasure Bound* (W.W. Norton & Company: New York, 2011)

MacCarthy, Fiona, *The Last Pre-Raphaelite* (Faber & Faber: London, 2011)

Mankowitz, Wolf, *Dickens of London* (Macmillan Publishing Co. Inc.: New York, 1976)

Moore, Wendy, *Wedlock* (Crown Publishers: New York, 2009)

Murphy, Emmett, *Great Bordellos of the World* (Quartet Books: London, 1983)

Obrien, Edna, *Byron in Love* (Weidenfeld & Nicolson: London, 2009)

Roiphe, Katie, *Uncommon Arrangements* (Dial Press: New York, 2007)

Rubenhold, Hallie, *The Lady in Red* (St Martin's Press: New York, 2008)

Slater, Michael, *Charles Dickens* (Yale University Press: New Haven & London, 2009)

Summerscale, Kate, *Mrs Robinson's Disgrace* (Bloomsbury: London, 2012)

Sutherland, John, *Lives of the Novelists* (Yale University Press: New Haven & London, 2012)

Tillyard, Stella, *A Royal Affair* (Chatto & Windus: London, 2006)

Tomalin, Claire, *Charles Dickens: A Life* (Penguin Press: New York, 2011)

Tomalin, Claire, *Thomas Hardy* (Penguin Press: New York, 2007)

Uglow, Jenny, *The Gambling Man* (Faber & Faber: London, 2009)

Vickery, Amanda, *Behind Closed Doors* (Yale University Press: New Haven & London, 2009)

Wood, Christopher, *The Pre-Raphaelites* (Weidenfeld & Nicolson: London, 1981)

Worsley, Lucy, *Courtiers: The Secrets of Kensington Palace* (Faber and Faber: London, 2010)

Wroe, Ann, *Being Shelley* (Pantheon Books: New York, 2007)

Index

If you enjoyed this book, you may also be interested in…

Gentlemen Rogues & Wicked Ladies: A Guide to British Highwaymen & Highwaywomen
Fiona McDonald
Everyone loves a romantic rogue whose exciting exploits feature a cheeky disregard for the law, narrow escapes and lots of love interest. There was the ever-courteous Claude du Vall, the epitome of gentlemanliness; and Dick Turpin, the most famous highwayman of them all. *Gentlemen Rogues* is an entertaining volume that will keep the reader glued to the page.
978-0-7524-6376-6

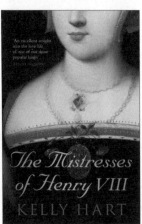

The Mistresses of Henry VIII
Kelly Hart
Henry VIII was considered a demi-god by his subjects, so each woman he chose had to stand out from the crowd, and those he selected were every bit as intriguing as the man himself. In this book, Henry's mistresses are rescued from obscurity and Kelly Hart gives an excellent insight into the love life of our most popular king, and the twelve women who knew the man behind the mask.
978-0-7524-5852-6

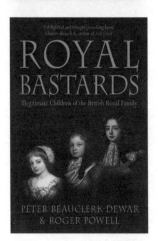

Royal Bastards: Illegitimate Children of the British Royal Family
Peter Beauclerk-Dewar & Roger Powell
Since 1066 when William the Conqueror took the throne English and Scottish kings have sired at least 150 children out of wedlock. Many were accepted at court and founded dynasties of their own. Others were barely acknowledged. This book is a genuinely fresh approach to British kings and queens, examining their lives and times through their illegitimate children.
978-0-7524-4668-4

Visit our website and discover thousands of other History Press books.

www.thehistorypress.co.uk